The Lord is . . .

The 2003 Christian Companion

The Lord is . . .
Published by Foundery Press

© Trustees Methodist Church Purposes, 2002
Cover picture photography:
   Landscape Light © Digital Vision Ltd

ISBN 1 85852 228 5

Compiled by Susan Hibbins

Printed in Great Britain by Stanley Hunt Limited

All rights reserved. No part of this publication may be reproduced, stored in a retrieval system, transmitted, in any form or by any means, electronic, mechanical, photocopying, recording or otherwise, without the prior permission of Foundery Press, 4 John Wesley Road, Werrington, Peterborough PE4 6ZP.

CONTENTS

Foreword
    Ian White

... the power of love's embrace   1
    Jonathan Sacks

... already before me   12
    Hilary Faith Jones

... inviting   21
    Francis Dewar

... saving his people   34
    Linda Hernandez

... the World's Most Incurable Optimist   44
    Timothy Wright

... a faithful and generous God   54
    Esther de Waal

... my refuge   63
    Angela Griffiths

... Lord of lords and King of kings   73
    Glennys Bamford

... the ultimate deliverer   82
    Michael Nazir-Ali

... closer than breathing   90
   Rachel Newton

... my inheritance   99
   Tom Taylor

... my guide and Father   110
   Andy Reed

... in the unknown future   119
   Albert Jewell

... with us on our journey   128
   Reg Bailey

... a God who heals   137
   Tony Trevithick

... there in the mess and turmoil of life   146
   Eluned Williams

... the strength of my heart   155
   Harold Good

... the source of life   165
   David Beazley

... worthy of praise   174
   Briant Smith

Contributors   181

Acknowledgements   189

FOREWORD

Where would you find a collection of thoughts, concerns and experiences that stem from a desire to speak with God? For me it would be the Book of Psalms. Within it is the story of a people in touch with God who are also seeking to understand what is happening around them. The Psalms show us a breadth of experience ranging from wonderful poetry and commitment to God to almost random thoughts. Some of these thoughts seem to be strung together, raising questions about God's relationship with the people – and theirs with God.

I often turn to the Psalms and derive great encouragement from them. Through Psalm 139 I am assured of God's continuing presence whatever the circumstances. In Psalm 84 there is refreshment in anticipation of sharing in worship. In the midst of my busyness I am challenged by Psalm 46.

It is a real joy to commend this *Companion* to you. From the experience of the contributors you will find refreshment for your journey. Out of their interpretation of the Psalms you will find new thoughts for your understanding and for your quiet reflection, and insight into God's continuing presence – even in the midst of turbulence.

I pray this collection of thoughts, reflections and experiences, based on the Psalms, will speak to you of God's love and grace – a true travelling Companion for today and for the future.

Ian T. White
President of the Methodist Conference, 2002-2003

... the power of love's embrace

Jonathan Sacks

Three memories. Anatoly – later Natan – Sharansky was one of the heroes of Soviet Jewry. For nine years he was held in prison and labour camps for the crime of wanting to leave Russia, go to Israel and live freely as a Jew. The long years of imprisonment, isolation and interrogation by the KGB might have broken his spirit, but they did not. Eventually he was set free and travelled to Israel, where he was reunited with his wife Avital and became a living symbol of those Russian-Jewish 'prisoners of hope' who had fought for and eventually won their freedom. When he was asked what kept him going, he took out from his pocket a little book. It had been given to him by Avital as he was taken by the Russian police and for nine years it had been his constant companion, his solace and source of strength. It was a book of Psalms.

The late Cardinal Hume was a transparent man of God. He radiated faith, and I cherished his friendship. Towards the end of his life, when he knew he had only months to live, I used to speak to him from time to time to see how he was, and if necessary lift his spirits. I never needed to. He was as serene in the face of death as he had been in life. I once asked him what was the source of his faith. His answer was simple: the Book of Psalms. Without it, he said, he could hardly imagine life. It was his oxygen, the air he breathed.

And then I think of my late father. Life was not easy for him. He had come to Britain as a child of five, fleeing persecution and anti semitism in Poland. His family was poor. At the age of 14 he had to leave school to help his father in business, and he always regretted the education he never had – and which he made sure we, his four sons, received. In his eighties he had to undergo a series of operations, each more debilitating than the last. What kept him going to the end was what he took with him each time to the hospital: a prayer shawl and phylacteries, a prayer book and a book of Psalms. He loved the Psalms, which he read in Hebrew. I was moved by his faith, simple and immensely strong. There were times when I would watch him read psalms and see him physically recover as if he had just had a good meal or a drink of whisky. The words were his injection of courage. They kept him from fear and despair. They sustained him through four surgical ordeals, and kept him company until the end.

What is it about the Book of Psalms that has given it its undiminished power through 30 centuries? Jews have long divided the Hebrew Bible into three: *Torah* (the Mosaic books, the Pentateuch), *Nevi'im* (the books of the prophets) and *Ketuvim* (the other 'writings', of which the Book of Psalms is one). In the first two, God speaks to humankind. In the third, humankind speaks to God. Jewish life has always been a dialogue between earth and heaven, sometimes majestic, at other times full of hurt and pain. Yet true relationships can survive the deepest trauma as long as the two parties continue to talk to one another and listen to one another. The Book of Psalms is our word to God in response to his word to us. It is as infinitely varied as human emotion itself – from praise to plea, from celebration to cry, from glory to something close to despair. But never despair itself, because the very fact that we can speak knowing that someone is listening is the ultimate rescue from despair. As one of the greatest of all Psalms puts it: 'Yea, though I walk through the valley of the shadow of death, I will fear no evil, for thou art with me' (AV). We can face anything if we know that we do not face it alone.

Psalm 8 is an unusual text, less emotional than philosophical. In a mere nine verses it expresses some of Judaism's deepest and most revolutionary beliefs. With rare exceptions, Jews did not write philosophical treatises. There is no counterpart, in our long history, to a Plato or an Aristotle, a Locke or David Hume. Even the greatest Jewish philosopher of all, Moses Maimonides, wrote his masterpiece, *The Guide for the Perplexed*, more as an afterthought – an extended letter to a troubled disciple – than as the central project of his life. It was the 11th-century poet Judah Halevi who best explained why. There is a difference, he said, between the God of Abraham and the God of Aristotle. The God of the philosophers is a concept. The God of the prophets is a person. About concepts, we think, but to persons, we speak. So when Jews reflected on God, the universe and humankind, they did so more through poetry and prayer than by way of philosophical systems. That is what Psalm 8 is: philosophy as prayer; reflection as praise. It is a fugue on the greatness of God and his image, humankind, constructed in a counterpoint of joy and awe.

The first thing the psalmist does is take us by surprise. I imagine him looking up at the sky on one of those dazzlingly clear nights you get in Jerusalem, stunned into silence by the star-filled sky. Immediately, though, he moves beyond the visible horizon. For the ancients the heavens were the arena of the gods. To the Mesopotamians they were where Anu, greatest of the gods, had his home. To the Eygptians they represented the divine mother through whom humankind was reborn. Today we know much more: that what we see is only the inner rim of a universe 18 billion light-years across containing more than a billion galaxies, each of more than a billion stars. Yet we still think of the universe as a limit, and wait for a message to reach us from some distant planet to tell us we are not alone under the unfeeling sky.

The psalmist thinks differently. The heavens themselves, inconceivably vast, are only 'the work of your fingers'. What a stunning metaphor! God is not within the universe but immeasurably beyond. He is not at the outermost limit of visibility to be discovered by some future Hubble space telescope. He is somewhere else, something else: not creation but Creator; not the world but the will that brings worlds into being.

Then comes the great leap, as unexpected today as it was 3,000 years ago. In theory, the vaster our conception of God, the smaller must be our sense of ourselves. Looking up at the stars, endless and eternal, most of us – our gaze turning inward – would think of our own insignificance. We live, we dream, we act, we die, leaving barely a footstep in the sands of time.

The psalmist realises that the opposite is true, and it is this astonishing idea that is the heart of his poem. If the universe were all there is, then we really are next to nothing. Our time is brief, our power circumscribed, our life significant only to ourselves. Nothing in nature seems to care. The same sun that shone when we were born will shine unmoved on the day we die. The winds howl, the storm rages, indifferent to the lives they shatter and the chaos they create.

But the universe is not all there is. Beyond it is God who summoned it into existence, who fashioned it in love, whose very being tells us that we are here because someone wanted us to be, who willed us into life and who therefore knows and cares that we are here. This is what fills the psalmist with astonishment and joy. You, God, architect of sea and sky, placed within this giant landscape *us* – human beings, tiny, vulnerable, yet capable of thinking, imagining, praying our way to your presence, hearing your voice beneath the silence, sensing your guiding hand in the seemingly random rush of events. Psalm 8 is the counter-voice to Hamlet's embittered dismissal of humankind:

> What a piece of work is man! How noble in reason! How infinite in faculty! In form, in moving, how express and admirable! In action how like an angel! In apprehension how like a god! The

beauty of the world! The paragon of animals! And yet, to me, what is this quintessence of dust?

The psalmist knows that the truth is opposite: not 'How great and yet so small', but 'How small and yet so great'. 'What are human beings that you are mindful of them . . . yet you have made them a little lower than God.'

The real masterstroke of the poem, though, is its opening image, one that has struck many commentators as obscure:
> You have set your glory above the heavens. Out of the mouths of babes and infants you have founded a bulwark.

The conventional verse-division of our Bibles, which ends one sentence with the word 'heavens' and then begins the next, tends to hide the fact that we have here an instance of parallelism, the basic structure of biblical verse. The author of the psalm has created one of the most arresting contrasts in all of religious literature. God's presence can be felt in two settings above all: the starry heavens and the not-yet articulate murmurings of a young child. The first makes sense to us. It is almost a cliché. The starlit sky reminds us of the vast forces that surround us. Only the later phrase about the heavens being the work of God's fingers rescues the image from banality and transforms it into a revolutionary rejection of myth. But how do we see God in an image of a child, the most vulnerable being in nature?

What the psalmist has done – it became one of the great themes of the Bible – is to realise that God is not simply a creator. He is a parent. God is not what scientists and philosophers have so often thought him to be: First Cause, Prime Mover, initiator of the Big Bang, the being of whom Stephen Hawking famously wrote that if we could construct unified theoretical physics we would 'know the mind of God'. God is not a scientist making universes in a test-tube, worlds in a laboratory. The closest we can come, the least inadequate metaphor, is to think of parents who bring a child into being in and through an act of love. As they hold their baby in their arms they sense, more than any of us do at any other time, the awe-inspiring mystery of human life, at once the product of its begetters and yet unmistakably something new, different, a centre of consciousness all its own, now so small and fragile but containing within itself the power to grow and discover and create and write its own chapter in the human story.

That, the poet intimates, is what we are to God, so small and insignificant, yet God holds us in his arms as does a parent his or her new-born child, and in that gesture is concentrated all the generative power of love itself and its embrace. If we once know that love, an echo of it stays with us through all the pain and fear, the doubts and crises, that life will one day bring. We are not alone in an unfeeling universe. And though our thoughts and words may sometimes seem like the babbling of a child, God knows, as does a parent, that in these inarticulate syllables we are reaching out to a presence that enfolds us. And as we look up to the sky at night, as a child looks up to the face of the one who holds it, we can begin to discern an answering smile, infinitely tender, telling us that we are here because someone brought us into being in love; and in the knowledge of that love is all the strength we need to feel at home in the universe, knowing that our lives matter, our hopes are not mere dreams, and that as we strive to make our world more gracious, something at the very heart of being responds to us as the hand of a parent reaches out to a child.

> *What are those values, those inward powers which go to the fashioning of a true life? I do not hesitate to say that the first is a real faith in a real God. To me that is the master-key of all fine and glad living. God is real. He is thinking of me just now. He watched by my pillow last night. He sees me as I am, and in spite of all he sees and knows, in spite of my foolish wandering and deliberate sinning, he loves me. Doesn't your heart take fire at the thought that this is what God really is? I know mine does. I believe in God as my loving Father and Friend.*
>
> *Alistair Maclean*

What is true in our highest moments is always true, and true now. I am what my Father has said to me to be. It matters not what others think of me. It matters not what I think of myself – only what God thinks of me is the real and the true.

F. Warburton Lewis

Love is more than a characteristic of God; it is his character.

Anonymous

God is with me now,
Closer than breathing,
And nearer than hands and feet.
God has made me for himself.
I come from God,
I belong to God,
I go to God.
God knows me,
God loves me,
God has a use for me
Now and for ever.

Anonymous

In choosing to live for God we discover that it is he who has chosen us. We tend to think that we are the ones who do all the deciding. But the more we live in the light of God's truth the more aware we become that it is he who stands at the centre of the universe, and not us. It is he who does the beckoning and he who is the source of the magnetic field drawing all men and women to himself.

James Jones

[The Psalms] touch the depths of human nature and experience and it is no accident that all the generations who have known them have responded to them and have found them fit their own need. They are songs of the human soul, timeless and universal: it is the sacred poets of Israel, more than any others, who have well and truly interpreted the spirit of humankind.

H. Wheeler Robinson

'The heavens declare the glory of God' but they do not enter so deeply into our souls as the still, small voice which we may hear in our own hearts when we are alone with him, which speaks to each one of us in a language addressed to us individually, with a significance which almost must be in a large degree incommunicable.

Caroline Stephenson

There is something in us, deeper than hands or feet, that finds the way to the Central Reality, and when we arrive we know it.

Rufus M. Jones

It is God who in his love commits himself completely to us, who adores us, who prays for us, dies for us, gives his heart to us, whether we respond or whether we don't. Here is a God who provides rain and sun on just and unjust, good and bad alike, a God who gives abundant love as a pure favour, completely free to the whole universe.

Michael Ball

Lead us into the silence that can both listen and hear,
Into the openness that can receive, into the rest that holds us on your way.
Lead us within the mystery of silence.
Help us to hear the great silence at the heart of God.
Help us to trust the eternal listener in silence, the mysterious presence at the heart of silence that sustains, enables, listens within and to the depths that we shall never exhaust or fathom.

Anonymous

True contemplation consists not in speculations concerning the mysteries of the Divine Being, but in fixing the anchor of thy thoughts in the deep sea of God's infinite love to humankind, with whom in heart and mind you must be united and incorporated, so as by and through his love to be purified and perfected.

Diego de Estella

> The human soul is a silent harp in God's choir, whose strings need only to be swept by the divine breath to chime in with the harmonies of creation.
>
> *Henry David Thoreau*

As the honey distils from the comb of the bees,
And the milk flows from the woman that loves her children;
So also is my hope on thee, my God.
As the fountain gushes out its water,
So my heart gushes out the praise of the Lord
And my lips utter praise to him,
And my tongue his psalms.
And my face exults with his gladness
And my spirit exults in his love,
And my soul shines in him,
And I trust in him.

> Odes of Solomon

The devout spirit in its ideal and perfection is a spirit completely filled with God. It sees him everywhere, in the order of nature, in the course of history, in the events of daily life. It knows itself to be in personal relation with him. It seeks to think his thoughts after him, and to know his will, and by them it chooses its tasks and shapes its steps. It is conscious of sharing God's life, his strength, his peace, his joy, his immortality. Its whole environment is God. The psalmist has expressed it once for all: 'Whom have I in heaven but thee? And there is none upon earth that I desire beside thee.'

> *J. Arundel Chapman*

... already before me

Hilary Faith Jones

I have sat and pondered many months,
ruminating in the back of my mind, to discover a psalm which struck a particular resonance within me.
My dilemma lay not in finding one but in wanting to share so many. Depending on my mood or my need, I found myself lingering over the psalms, forgetting that the shadows lengthened as I stepped into the land of exquisite songs.
I have always been staggered by the poetry of the psalmists,
amazed at the profundity within their verses;
delighted by the richness and vividness of the imagery.
And somewhere, deep inside, a longing to return to using such beauty within our everyday language.
Just so, in church services it is never a chore to share in the congregational psalm from the back of the Methodist hymn book – it is always a pleasure – for many times I have found my eyes drifting back to reread a verse that has caught my imagination.

The psalm I want to share with you is one that I have puzzled over and returned to in times of sorrow,
and quiet thought,
and in times of challenge when nothing in life has seemed straightforward.
It is Psalm 139, 'O Lord, you have searched me and known me!'
It is to me a most beautiful song of wonder being poured out to God.
And at the same time, it is the most intimate prayer.
Yet within it are verses of deep resentment – indeed of hatred.

I have to admit that I enjoy the congregational version of the psalm more than the biblical reading, for it omits v19-22. But maybe this is a cop-out. Maybe the words that seem filled with vengeance and vitriol can teach me. Sometimes to be challenged to look further and dig deeper for explanations helps to shed a new insight on that which I would rather too readily dismiss.

So to my love for this psalm.
It strikes me from the very first words that this is an unusually intimate conversation between myself and God.
It is a frank acknowledgement to God.
It is an offering of truth and wonder.
And most wonderfully of all,
it is a realisation that God is so deeply a part of my being,
that we are woven intrinsically together as one.

God was there at my creation.
God brought me into being – and placed me in this time.
If he is in all places,
from the highest heavens to the darkest deaths, from the wideness of the morning's light to the deepest seas,
he is already part of my thinking,
part of my actions,
part of my speech.
God is intimately within *me* – as I am intimately within him.

I move, live, breathe within the creation of God.

Gosh – that's some thought! And one which I find hard to hold in my mind. It is too big for me to even catch hold of the edges.

And then, quite unexpectedly, I see glimpses of this profundity –
a father leaning out to guide his child across the road,
a chance laughter between lovers,
two elderly sisters completing each other's sentences,

broken bread,
arms wide open.

As the thought catches and tugs at my understanding,
at the same time it is deeply enriching.
Why!
I do not need to put clumsy human words into explanations,
I do not need to go home to be asked what is wrong –
God *already* knows – and understands.
God is already before me –
a part of my delight,
or my searching,
or my sorrow.

But then, what of those verses that I do not understand?
The psalmist so full of hate towards his enemies,
so humanly longing for retribution,
so achingly wanting divine intervention.
If I think of them in the context of the Easter truth, it helps me to approach the words from a new angle.
What time, what energy was given up by the psalmist to be consumed by such thoughts!
Time in which God could have been breathed in.
Wouldn't it be awful if I too wasted precious moments being swamped by hatred;
And wouldn't it be awful if I was the knowing cause of anger –
and thus destroyed another's life?

So sometimes I read the psalm as it is found in the Bible – and use those verses to put my life back into perspective.
And yes, I do read and reread those first 18 verses, especially vv17 and 18:

> How weighty to me are your thoughts, O God!
> How vast is the sum of them!
> I try to count them – they are more than the sand;
> I come to the end – I am still with you.
> When I hit the lowest,

I hold tight to those words –
and whisper them again and again in my heart –
That God thought of me,
even before I was formed,
that he continues to think of me –
and will never cease to think about me –
beyond the end of time.

That makes life worth living.

We cannot form an adequate concept of [humanity] unless we include God. He is mysterious, transcendent and ineffable, the eternal principle of the universe. But he watches over us, knows and observes us, and preserves us unceasingly.

Pope Paul VI

The light of God surrounds me,
The love of God enfolds me,
The power of God protects me,
The presence of God watches over me,
Wherever I am, God is.

Catherine Marshall

God is an unutterable sigh in the innermost depths of the soul.

Anonymous

To love God is to see traces of him everywhere.

G. H. Morrison

Grace comes into the soul as the morning sun into the world; first a dawning, then a light, and at last the sun in his full excellent brightness.

Thomas Adams

> In every heart he wishes to be first;
> He therefore keeps the secret key himself
> To open all its chambers, and to bless
> With perfect sympathy, and holy peace,
> Each solitary soul which comes to him.
>
> Source unknown

God in the heavens is more my heaven than the heavens themselves; in the sun he is more my light than the sun; in the air he is more my air than the air I breathe sensibly. He works in me all that I am, all that I see, all that I do or can do, as most intimate, most present, and most immanent in me.

Louis Chardon

O Lord, when I awake, and day begins,
    waken me to thy Presence;
    waken me to thine indwelling;
    waken me to inward sight of thee
        and speech with thee,
            and strength from thee;
    that all my earthly walk may waken into song
        and my spirit leap up to thee all day, all ways.

O my God,
    all times are thy times,
    and every day thy day,
made lovely only with thy light.
Bring us, O Lord, to that blessed eternal day
        which thy Son our Saviour hath won for us,
        and to the perfect light.

Eric Milner-White

As the sun, rising in the morning, shines into thy house if thou dost but open thy windows, so God, the unsleeping king, will shine in upon the soul which unfolds itself to him; for God, like the sun above us, is ready to enter within each of us if we open unto him.

St John of the Cross

Go as high as you can, go as deep as you can, fly as far east as the sunrise, or westwards to the limit of the sea – and God is still there. There is no experience of life in which he does not confront you. He confronts you in the heavenly experiences, and the times that you call 'sheer hell', in the freshness of new experiences, those that are like the dawn, and the time of life when the sun is setting in the west. In all of them God finds you and confronts you with his challenges and disturbances, and his strength and peace.

Kenneth Slack

Lord God Almighty, I pray thee for thy great mercy and by the token of the holy rood,
Guide me to thy will, to my soul's need, better than I can myself;
And shield me against my foes, seen and unseen;
And teach me to do thy will
That I may inwardly love thee before all things with a clean mind and a clean body.
For thou art my maker and my redeemer,
My help, my comfort, my trust and my hope.
Praise and glory be to thee now, ever and ever, world without end.

King Alfred

When God created this world and humanity, God intended that we should be free lovers whose choices arise from free decision, not mechanical puppets with no alternatives. God has taken enormous risks to create such a world in which we are free to choose, free to make mistakes. But would any other way have had any significant meaning at all? God has entered into the costs of this risk. God does not stand about, observing. While we make mistakes, learn, grow, struggle, refuse or consent to love, use or abuse our freedom, God's heart shares the full experience.

Flora Slosson Wuellner

Take comfort, and recollect however little you and I may know, God knows; he knows himself and you and me, and all things; and his mercy is over all his works.

Charles Kingsley

God goes before us. We don't know the way, but he does; every inch of it. He prepared it, appointed it, and has trodden it. That is enough. I don't know where I am going, but I know I am going with him.

Samuel Chadwick

... inviting

Francis Dewar

In one of his books, Thomas Merton describes a summer dawn in the valley where his monastery was set. When they rise for the night office at two-fifteen in the morning there is no sound except in the monastery. By three there are the first stirrings of the birds in the valley. He writes:

> The first chirps of the waking day birds mark the *point vierge* of the dawn under a sky as yet without real light, a moment of awe and inexpressible innocence, when the Father in perfect silence opens their eyes. They begin to speak to Him, not with fluent song, but with an awakening question that is their dawn state, their state at the *point vierge*. Their condition asks if it is time for them to *be*. He answers 'yes'. Then they one by one wake up and become birds. They manifest themselves as birds, beginning to sing. Presently they will be fully themselves, and will even fly.

'All wisdom,' he writes, 'seeks to collect and manifest itself at that blind sweet point . . . the virgin point between darkness and light, between non-being and being.' It is a lovely image, a metaphor of God's invitation to every human being, his calling you into being and inviting you to sing your song.

In this brief article I shall be suggesting you set this beside Psalm 119, as a Christian way to read the psalm. At first sight this may sound pretty improbable; the psalm looks as though it is saying the exact opposite. Almost every verse speaks of the law, the commandments, the testimonies, the statutes, the judgements of God. It sounds as though it is all about rules, as though a godly life consisted simply in keeping a set of injunctions laid down by God. Where is grace, in a psalm that is so enthusiastic about the law? Where is the gospel in that?

In the Epistle to the Galatians St. Paul writes, 'Before faith came, we were imprisoned and guarded under the law . . . the law was our disciplinarian until Christ came . . . But now that faith has come, we are no longer subject to a disciplinarian, for in Christ Jesus you are all children of God through faith' (3:23-26). I think it is helpful to understand what he says, not just in terms of the corporate history of our religion, Judaism leading into Christianity, but in terms of each individual person's development from childhood to mature adulthood. Each of us, when we are young, are 'under the law'. We are loaded up with instructions: 'Do it this way', 'Never do that'; all kinds of 'oughts' and 'shoulds' – 'This is the way to live/behave/grow/earn your living.' Like camels we carry quite a heavy load of packages, parcels, bags, boxes, suitcases, trunks, packing cases. That is part of the civilising and socialising process that we all need to go through when we are young.

But, as St. Paul says in Galatians, obeying the rules only brings you to the threshold of life: it does not lift you over it. If you go through the whole of your life as a camel, you are 'under the law', never maturing into self-responsible adulthood. An adult needs to be able to go beyond the mere keeping of rules, to be free enough to take risks, to be able to love generously and to be creative. The process of growing up requires adolescence, when the rules are challenged and luck is pushed. The camel needs to become a lion: because, in Nietzsche's metaphor (and these animal images are his), only the strength of a lion can do battle with the fearsome dragon whose name is 'thou shalt', and on whose every scale all over his body is inscribed in gold the words *thou shalt*. If the dragon prevails, nothing new or creative is possible. The lion has to slay him. But having done that, the lion cannot create newness of itself: all the lion achieves by that is to make newness possible. The lion, says Nietzsche, needs to become a child, at play, without preconceptions, a 'self-propelling wheel', a sacred 'yes'.

It's an illuminating image, the three stages of growing up in spirit, camel, lion and adult 'child', and very relevant to understanding Psalm 119. It is a marvellous psalm, but widely misunderstood by the camels of this world. In its original Old Testament context it is, of course, speaking about the Jewish law and about the strict observance of it. It reminds me of my own camelhood, which lasted well into my 40s! The Christianity that my parents laid upon me was entirely about doing your duty. And somehow there hung in the air a whisper that it definitely wasn't going to be something you enjoyed doing; it was about the cross, about doing things you didn't want to do. It was loveless, heavy and burdensome (in actual fact a perversion of what the cross is about). One of the people whose writing helped me to grow out of being a camel was Elizabeth O' Connor. A sentence of hers that I came across in the 70s is still engraved on my heart: 'We ask to know the will of God without guessing that his will is written into our very beings.' This is the way to read Psalm 119, as an adult 'child' rather than a camel. I discovered that the 'law' of God is not something alien, imposed from without on an unwilling heart: it is the deepest law of my being, the enactment of which is joy, fulfilment and life, for myself and for some others.

As I write this there is a song thrush in a tree outside my window singing its heart out. That is its nature, to trill and to pipe its lovely repeated phrases into space. It is enacting the law, the commandments, the statutes, the testimonies of its being. Each of us, similarly, is invited by God to sing our song for others (metaphorically, of course – you don't have literally to be a musician). For one, it may be something you do in your spare time, something you love to do, something which is rooted in your very centre, in your heart of hearts, which gives service or freedom or delight to others. For another it will be something that has the same feel about it that you do at work, something beyond what the job spec. requires, or some aspect of the job that you feel you can put your whole heart and soul into in your own unique way. If that is the case with you, you are fortunate, because many, perhaps most, feel they are obliged to sing someone else's song, to dance to someone else's tune. There's nothing wrong with that in some aspects of your life. But when that is true of all your existence, it is dehumanising, destructive both of your own spirit and of those who are around you.

However, discovering what *your* song is to be can be quite difficult. We live in a world where most expect their song to be handed to them by someone else. Not only does that happen rarely: I suspect it never happens. Your true song is something that is much more idiosyncratic than that, something that has roots deep in your nature, in your personal history, in your circumstances, in your capabilities, in your disabilities, and in the suffering you have encountered – your own and others'. All sorts of personal factors mean that the song you 'write', and the people that it is for, has something unique about it, not copied or taken from someone else. There is much personal dragon-slaying to be done before the untrammelled adult child can emerge, full of life, seeing without preconceptions, self-motivating, at play in the world in your capacity for lateral thinking, inventive experimenting, and plunging into action generously and riskily for others.

I am talking about vocation. It is a much-misused word. In the Church it has been hijacked by the clergy. In the wider world it long ago became narrowed to mean 'profession', something only the highly-educated and well qualified could aspire to. It was further devalued to mean good paid employment. Now it has been totally debased to mean any old slot of wage-slave existence – in such phrases as 'vocational training'. The word vocation has become drained of red blood, purged of passion and emptied of God. It badly needs to be restored to its full meaning: it is *God's* invitation to you to *live*. It is your *life*, a gift of God to you, in the enacting of which you become a gift to others. And it is for everyone, for every human being. God invites everyone to offer something unique to the life of the world, something which only you can do: and which, if you don't do it, will for ever remain undone.

There are many aspects to the discerning of your personal vocation, and it can be a long process spread over decades, not least because it is often only by trial and error that you discover what you are *not* for. A good starting point might be to ask yourself, 'What is my passion?' What are you passionate about? Newts? Astronomy? Cars? Clothes? Stamp collecting? Dancing? To answer this question alone needs a bit of discernment. What is the difference between an interest, a fad, an obsession, an enthusiasm, and a passion? These words cover a wide spectrum. By a passion I mean something that touches your innermost heart and soul. Many of us are out of touch with our inmost selves, for all sorts of reasons which are not necessarily our fault. You may have to have lived for several decades before you discover what you are really passionate about. Of course, a passion of yours will not necessarily be your vocation: there are many other matters to explore in the discernment of that. But the task or tasks that God calls you to will be something that you discover you are passionate about, something that genuinely engages your very heart and soul.

Other important questions in discovering your personal calling from God are 'What service will you give?' 'Who will what you do be for?' 'To whom might it be a gift?' 'In what way?' Vocation is not just about self-fulfilment; it is a call to do something which will be a gift to others, directly or indirectly. It is about offering your very self in action for others.

St. Paul had a special word for personal vocation, *kharis* in Greek, translated 'grace'. He writes, 'This grace was given to me, to bring to the Gentiles the news of the boundless riches of Christ' (Ephesians 3:8). That was Paul's description of his personal vocation. *Kharis* is an unusually multi-faceted word, and contains within it much of the richness of the notion of personal vocation. It can mean grace of form or speech, attractiveness, gracefulness. It can mean a feeling of favourable regard towards someone. It can mean a favour, as in 'doing a favour' to someone. It can mean gratitude, the feeling produced by receiving a favour. And finally, in an adverbial form, it means 'for the sake of'. All these meanings are true of personal vocation. When someone is doing what they're born for, there is an attractive, captivating, heart-warming quality about what they do. When you are doing what you are for, it feels an enormous privilege, quite unmerited, evoking deep gratitude. And what you are and what you do is for the sake of someone else, probably some particular people.

Psalm 119 is the psalm of personal vocation.

Blessed, deeply blest, *are those who walk in the law of the Lord* (v1), who walk in the law of their deepest being:

I have taken greater delight in the way of your testimonies than in all manner of riches (v14)

Your statutes have been like songs to me (v54)

Your testimonies are wonderful (v129)

Therefore I love your commandments above gold, even much fine gold (v127)

It is good for me that I have been afflicted, that I may learn your statutes (v71):

> very commonly someone's personal calling arises from something they have regarded as a problem, or a disability, or handicap, or trauma, or disaster, which they have come to some sort of terms with.

The proud have dug pits for me (v85)

They draw nigh that in malice persecute me (v150)

> When you are doing what you are born for it can be threatening to others, particularly to those who are not doing what they're for, and who pursue substitutes like security or status, money or possessions. What you do will disturb the status quo, injure some sensitive egos, threaten some power structures.

I have gone astray like a sheep that is lost; O seek your servant, for I do not forget your commandments (v176)

O that my ways were made steadfast in keeping your statutes (v5):

> I am not always faithful to your call and go wandering off: don't let me go, you are my life, responding to your call to me is my deepest joy.

I am as glad of your word as one who finds great spoils (v162)

> The word of God calls you into existence and lays down the law of your being. 'The Lord called me before I was born, while I was in my mother's womb he named me,' says Isaiah (49:1).

The sower sows the word, says Jesus (Mark 4:14). The word is not the Bible. It is not some general pronouncement of universal application. It is God's word to each human being, uniquely and personally, God's invitation to live and to be fruitful in some specific way. Jesus points to the ways in which the germination and growth of the seed is prevented or hindered. Satan removes it. Or it grows too rapidly without root – enthusiasm is not enough; if it is not rooted deeply in your heart and soul, you will not be able to cope with the hassle and ill-will it may bring you. Or the cares of the world, and the lure of wealth, and the desire of other things come in and choke the word. Jesus understood only too well how that can happen, and he is, of course, *the* example of personal vocation. The parable of the sower was taken from his own experience. In his temptations in the desert he felt the power of the things that might lure him aside, divert him from his passion and joy, annul the law of his being, block his response to God's call. That time in the desert was the necessary prelude to his wholehearted and passionate giving of himself in the story-telling, teaching and healing of the first years of his ministry.

When you have an opportunity, give yourself some 'desert' time, time apart to listen to your inmost longings, to open your heart to the needs of others, and hear what God might be inviting from you. And when you get into action may you discover in Psalm 119 a faithful and truthful companion.

> *Live your life while you have it. Life is a splendid gift. There is nothing small in it. For the greatest things grow by God's law out of the smallest. You must not fritter it away . . . but you must make your thoughts, your words, your acts, all work to the same end, and that end not self, but God.*
>
> *Florence Nightingale*

Each day, each week, each month, each year, is a new chance given you by God. A new chance, a new leaf, a new life – this is the golden, the unspeakable gift which each day offers you.

F. W. Farrar

*Let us take hands and help, this day we are alive together,
Look up on high and thank the God of all.*

On a bench in Kew Gardens

Follow the path that you know to be right, whatever your doubts may be about what you call the unseen. And as you follow, persistently, faithfully, you will come to be sure of something else too. You will come to feel that the voice calling you along that path is not simply your own voice. It is not the beating of your own heart you are hearing. It is the beating of the heart of the universe. It comes through what you call your own conscience, yet it comes as the voice of the Infinite . . . In other words you will come to be sure that those ideals of purity, honesty, courage and love are but the shadowings of an unseen realm in which they are perfectly realised, a kingdom of love; a king of love, a God whom you can absolutely trust.

D. M. Baillie

Every person can help on the world's work more than they know of. What we want is the single eye, that we may see what our work is, the humility to accept it, however lowly, the faith to do it for God, the perseverance to go on till death.

Norman Macleod

True ambition is a deep desire to live usefully and walk humbly in the grace of God.

Anonymous

How can you give God anything when he owns everything? But does he? How about that power to choose, that precious free-will that he has given to every living personality and which he so greatly respects? That is the only present we can give – ourselves, with all our powers of spirit, mind and body – willingly, freely, given because we love him. That is the best and highest worship that you and I can offer, and I am sure that it is this above all that God most highly appreciates.

J. B. Phillips

I am trying to make it more and more a guiding thought in my own life that God is working his purpose out in it. This thought gives much relief from all anxiety as to ultimate success, or avoidance of all failure, and all fear as to wasting one's life. Do we not believe in God? And a God who is supremely concerned in our own life-work and who will assuredly guide it according to his divine plan, if we allow him?

W. T. Gardiner

If you believe in the Lord, he will do half the work – but the last half. He helps those who help themselves.

Cyrus K. Curtis

Live as with God, and whatever be your calling, pray for the gift that will perfectly qualify you in it.

Horace Bushnell

> Here in a quiet and dusty room they lie,
> Faded as crumbled stone or shifting sand,
> Forlorn as ashes, shrivelled, scentless, dry –
> Meadows and gardens running through my hand.
>
> In this brown husk a dale of hawthorn dreams,
> A cedar in this narrow cell is thrust;
> That will drink deeply of a century's streams,
> These lilies shall make summer on my dust.
>
> Here in their safe and simple house of death,
> Sealed in their shells a million roses leap;
> Here I can blow a garden with my breath,
> And in my hand a forest lies asleep.
>
> Muriel Stuart

To accomplish great things, we must not only act but also dream, not only plan but also believe.

Anatole France

Part of the answer of every prayer is the grace to need and ask for something else . . . The vision of the true wealth, the sense of life's spiritual possibility, grows clearer and deeper with the fuller coming of the heavenly kingdom into our lives.

Percy Ainsworth

Give to the world the best you have, and the best will come back to you.

Anonymous

God is to me that creative Force, behind and in the universe, who manifests himself as energy, as life, as order, as beauty, as thought, as conscience, as love.

Henry Sloane Coffin

God does not ask about our ability or our inability, but our availability.

Anonymous

... saving his people

Linda Hernandez

When I was a child, it didn't occur to me that anyone actually read the Bible for pleasure, except perhaps the preachers I saw up in the pulpit on Sundays. I just assumed that most people simply kept a Bible in their home as a reference book – rather like a dictionary or a first-aid book – to be referred to only occasionally.

Having been brought up in the Christian faith, it seemed only natural to become a church member when I was a teenager. That was back in the late 1960s, a time when many people were questioning and rejecting traditional values and teachings and it felt very 'uncool' to be a Christian.

In my late teens I was not immune to the newspaper articles and television programmes which argued so persuasively against Christianity. I only ever seemed to meet Christians on a Sunday, inside a church – never on a weekday at college or at work. Worse still: to my young eyes, the weekday world seemed to be doing 'very nicely, thank you' without God. It was puzzling and I gave the matter a lot of thought, drifting further away from regular church attendance in the process, but still considering myself to be a Christian.

Then, one Easter, I nearly lost my faith in God completely. A voice on the radio was describing Jesus' agony on the cross, and as I listened to the poignant words, 'My God, my God, why have you forsaken me?', a terrifying thought crossed my mind. Supposing Jesus had discovered there was no God? This seemed a very rational possibility, even though I didn't like the idea! As a result, I found myself in a spiritual desert for the next few years, yearning for an oasis.

With hindsight, I see now that the Holy Spirit was imperceptibly guiding me onwards. After moving to a new town with my husband, I found myself joining a new church and taking my toddler and baby to Sunday school on a regular basis. However, I remained a rather uncommitted churchgoer for several more years until one day I was invited to join a new Bible study group and it occurred to me I might just find an answer to that question which had been bothering me over the years.

If only I had known how to study the Bible properly 25 years earlier! One week, our group was asked to read a selection of psalms at home between meetings and that particular week I read from a modern translation which – for me – gave the words particular impact. For the first time in my life I read Psalm 22, which is both a cry of anguish and a song of praise. To my amazement, it opened with the words that Jesus uttered on the cross! How could this be – it was written many centuries earlier!

As I began to read, I realised that the psalmist was begging God to deliver him from terrible anguish. He received no sympathy from the people around him: they were expecting him to die, and were already dividing his clothes between themselves. Yet through his pain and anguish he was nevertheless able to perceive the Lord, to trust in him, and finally to praise him, in the certainty that he has dominion over all, now and for ever.

Psalms are faith poetry, and faith poetry is a personal reflection on God. Countless generations have found comfort, reassurance and hope in Psalm 22 and it can still be so for present-day readers and for people in generations to come. What a tremendous psalm for someone alone at night, feeling unloved and fearing death; for the terminally ill; for those in desperate mental anguish or simply overwhelmed by life's many problems. Surely those of us who have found ourselves blessed through the words of Psalm 22 should remember to share them whenever we come across others who are seeking comfort, reassurance and hope. As v5 tells us:

> In you they trusted, and were not put to shame.

On that level alone, Psalm 22 is magnificent. But this psalm has far greater dimensions: it foretells the agony of Christ on the cross. Tears were streaming down my face as I read it for the first time. Verses 14 and 15 are immensely moving and at that point I could scarcely continue reading:

> I am poured out like water,
> and all my bones are out of joint;
> my heart is like wax;
> it is melted within my breast;
> my mouth is dried up like a potsherd,
> and my tongue sticks to my jaws;
> you lay me in the dust of death.

At v18, a cold chill went down my spine as I read:

> They divide my clothes among themselves,
> and for my clothing they cast lots.

This vividly brings to mind the description of the Roman soldiers at the foot of the cross centuries later, who are mentioned in the Gospels of Mark, Luke and John. We are told in 2 Timothy 3:16 and 17 that 'all Scripture is inspired by God', and instances such as this really heighten our awareness of that fact.

Surely God inspired the psalmist to depict an event which exemplified the human condition as experienced (perhaps by the psalmist himself) at that particular moment in history, and which was also to be experienced centuries later by Jesus. During his ministry Jesus quoted Scripture on several occasions, illustrating that the Messianic texts had found their fulfilment in him.

What had once seemed to me a rational explanation of the words of Jesus had simply been taken out of their full context. Jesus' apparent question of despair in the midst of his agony had, in fact, been the opening lines of a specific psalm which began in anguish but ended in the certain knowledge of the love and power of God, which ever has been and will be for evermore. As God in human form, Jesus was subjected to the breaking point of human existence and yet – in the face of temptation to despair – Jesus uttered the opening words of a psalm which break through physical and mental anguish to the presence of God.

> But you, O Lord, do not be far away!
> O my help, come quickly to my aid.
> (v19)

Jesus was imparting a final and triumphant passage of Scripture to his followers – not only those present at Golgotha and in Jerusalem that day, but to all his followers down through the next 2,000 years to the 21st century and on throughout the rest of time!

> In you our ancestors trusted;
> they trusted, and you delivered them.
> (v4)

Psalm 22 closes with the certainty and reassurance that:
> ... all the families of the nations shall
> worship before him.
> Posterity will serve him;
> future generations will be told about the Lord,
> and proclaim his deliverance to a people yet
>   unborn,
> saying that he has done it.
> (v27, 30-31)

Each time I reread this psalm, it becomes more and more awe-inspiring as I contemplate the wondrous vision which it imparts to a reader who is seeking the Lord. So often we worry about the future of Christianity in the western world and there is often talk at present of the rapid decline of the church in this country. How wonderful to have the assurance of Jesus that future generations will serve God and that people not yet born will be told the Good News.

I have at last found the glorious, overwhelming answer to that question which had troubled me for so long. Thanks be to God.

In the diary of many people's lives there have been oases and resting places. 'When I was hard-pressed, he came to my rescue' (Psalm 4:1). Certainly there may have been times of great sorrow and deep suffering but it is the experience of faith that it is precisely within those periods of darkness and wilderness that God's faithfulness is made plain . . . It is important never to forget what God has done in the past for the past points to the surety of God to be God in the present and the future. The contour of God is enabling in time of challenge, and faithful in the story of the past.

Anthony Hulbert

Give me, O Lord, a steadfast heart,
which no unworthy thought can drag downwards,
an unconquered heart, which no tribulation can wear out;
an upright heart, which no unworthy purpose may tempt aside.
Bestow upon me also, O Lord my God, understanding to know thee,
diligence to seek thee,
wisdom to find thee,
and a faithfulness that may finally embrace thee;
through Jesus Christ our Lord.

St. Thomas Aquinas

Jesus understood who he was and what he was called to become by praying the psalms . . . The psalms, infused with this presence of Christ, make accessible and actual for us the full range of Jesus' experience. In praying the psalms, we enter into that world of meaning and find our own wilderness sojourn illuminated and clarified. In praying the psalms we pass through our own hearts to the heart of God as revealed in Jesus' inner life.

Thomas R. Hawkins

God will not permit any troubles to come upon us, unless he has a specific plan by which great blessing can come out of the difficulty.

Peter Marshall

We know then that joy is the sweetness of contact with the love of God, that affliction is the wound of this same contact when it is painful, and that only matters, not the manner of it . . . The knowledge of this presence of God does not afford consolation, it takes nothing from the fearful bitterness of affliction, nor does it heal the mutilation of the soul. But we know quite certainly that God's love for us is the very substance of this bitterness and this mutilation. I should like out of gratitude to be able to bear witness to this.

Simone Weil

> *I weave a silence on to my lips*
> *I weave a silence into my mind*
> *I weave a silence within my heart*
> *I close my ears to distractions*
> *I close my eyes to attractions*
> *I close my heart to temptations.*
>
> *Calm me, O Lord, as you stilled the storm*
> *Still me, O Lord, keep me from harm*
> *Let all tumult within me cease*
> *Enfold me, Lord, in your peace.*
>
> *David Adam*

The solid ground of hope in the Old Testament lies not in past history, nor in the prospect of future blessing, but lies in God, who is known as the God of truth. The urge to hope is not just a snare to lure Israel to a promised land of nothing but sinking sand. The hope of Israel sprang from their conviction that God's word is the truth; and the truth is that he has so made his world that his people can have hope in this life.

Wilfred Easton

Prayer is a cry of hope.

French proverb

Thank God for tears,
the tears that flow unchecked,
that run in rivulets down to the sea of God;
that have to merge eventually
with something larger than the self.

Thank God for tears,
the tears that bring release
for knotted nerves
twisted as sinews,
bringing a breathing out
beyond despair.

Thank God for tears,
and then beyond the tears,
beyond the hopelessness
that has to offer up the grief
till no more fall,
because no more can fall –

the tiny step that is a journey's start,
a slow step onward,
numb at first and seemingly dead,
where haltingly, but gradually
one grassblade starts to grow
watered by tears;
somehow a kind of healing can begin.

Cecily Taylor

Here is the last great certainty. Be sure of God. With simple, loving worship, by continual obedience, by purifying yourself as he is pure, creep close to him, keep close to him. Be sure of God, and nothing can overthrow you.

Phillips Brooks

O Lord, calm the waves of this heart; calm its tempests. Calm thyself, O my soul, so that the divine can act in thee. Calm thyself, O my soul, so that God is able to repose in thee, so that his peace may cover thee. Yes, Father in heaven, often have we found that the world cannot give us peace; O but make us feel that thou art able to give peace; let us know the truth of thy promise: that the whole world may not be able to take away thy peace.

Soren Kierkegaard

Leave God to order all thy ways,
And hope in him whate'er betide;
Thou'll find him in the evil days
Thy all-sufficient strength and guide:
Who trusts in God's unchanging love
Builds on the rock that naught can move.

Sing, pray, and swerve not from his ways
But do thine own part faithfully;
Trust his rich promises of grace,
So shall they be fulfilled in thee:
God never yet forsoook at need
The soul that trusted him indeed.

George Neumark (tr. Catherine Winkworth)

... the World's Most Incurable Optimist

Timothy Wright

There are men and women enthusiastic about monastic life and they are young. They are enthusiastic about the very idea of entering a monastery. There may not be many of them, but that does not matter. What does matter is that enthusiasm. Where does it come from?

You may have looked round the ruins of ancient monasteries, or read the tales, often less than edifying, of what dwellers in those buildings are reported to have got up to, or you may have pondered monastic rules, aware that life in monasteries is unfashionably austere, boringly regular and offers no career path. It does not pretend to be anything else.

You may never have met a monk, or visited a living monastery, or heard monastic music, but let me assure you that there are people today enthusiastic about its purpose. Why? Because at its heart is a Lord, who is the World's Most Incurable Optimist.

At monastic profession, the candidate quotes v116 from Psalm 119: 'Uphold me according to your promise that I may live, and let me not be put to shame in my hope.' That verse, from the longest psalm in the Bible, was chosen by Benedict of Nursia, author of a Rule written about 500AD, to express succinctly and clearly the motive behind those proceeding to lifelong commitment in the monastery. From that one verse comes enthusiasm for monastic living. It deserves further development.

Let us look first at the context. The preceding verses go as follows:

> I hate the double-minded, but I love your law. You are my hiding-place and my shield. I hope in your word. Go away from me, you evildoers, that I may keep the commandments of my God.

The author of these words is faced with a choice and feels under pressure. Those around give little encouragement. Faith is not important to them. But their half-hearted faith and their disregard of the law of God reveals the psalmist's vulnerability. The writer feels horribly alone, with no real support from family or friends. The options are limited. The call to God is a desperate last ditch chance of survival; it recognises that only God provides guaranteed shelter, support, protection and hope. The commands of God shine brightly, like a searchlight in a darkened sky. Those who always look to the ground do not see it. But once seen and experienced the light makes all the difference. Only God, the World's Most Incurable Optimist, offers enough light to see where we stand and the direction in which we should walk. Truly we have something to be enthusiastic about.

Now let us turn to the verses immediately following Benedict's selected verse:

> Hold me up, that I may be safe and have regard for your statutes continually. You spurn all who go astray from your statutes; for their cunning is in vain. All the wicked of the earth you count as dross; therefore I love your decrees. My flesh trembles for fear of you, and I am afraid of your judgements.

After the first two lines, the mood changes. The light focuses on the stubbornness of those who refuse obedience, lead double lives, or are nasty to their neighbour. The Lord will discard them. That instills fear and trembling into the hearts of the follower too. It is a risky path; we are all tempted to adjust the commands of God to our own needs.

Together those eight verses from Psalm 119 offer an image of the spiritual life. We feel, in turn, weak, trusting, under threat, full of fear, crushed by the impossible, and, occasionally, lifted up by the support of the Lord.

Benedict's crucial verse summarises our position: 'Uphold me according to your promise, that I may live, and let me not be put to shame in my hope.' Unpacking it we see the central truths of monastic life. They are central in the lives of everyone: longing for something better, a life of repeated failure, continual pleas for help. The monastic life is, after all, just another way of Christian living.

As we ponder this, two elements stand out: first, the desire to dedicate our life to something really worthwhile, where the path is clearly laid out and the distractions removed, and second, the availability of God, the World's Most Incurable Optimist, each moment of the day, giving support and guidance, nudging us into ways that are practical and realistic.

For some the desire and the presence come together to create an energy which means the person is satisfied with nothing less than total commitment to a life in which the Lord is dominant in a single-minded, totally absorbing way. From this derives the enthusiasm for monastic living.

Once in the monastery, even within the first month, the novice's enthusiasm faces its first challenge. This enthusiasm has nothing to do with the Lord and all to do with that very human dream, that one would sense in the monastery, at every moment, the real presence of the Lord.

As the dream disappears, enthusiasm is threatened: 'Uphold me according to your promise, that I may live.' That short sentence takes on a new meaning. The novice's first lesson is to discover that true enthusiasm comes only from the Lord. The Lord does not live in the dream.

The longer we live, the more we realise how feeble we are. Frequent failure hinders progress but also reveals the extraordinary tolerance of the Lord. There is only one conclusion: the Lord is the World's Most Incurable Optimist. Out of the weakness of human nature, the Lord can bring forth great gifts in the most unexpected ways, gifts available free, without qualification. We simply have to stop ourselves ignoring, rejecting, or misusing them. Only a Lord who is an Incurable Optimist would present things in that way. Our psalmist says it all: let me not be put to shame in my hope. Even the most wasteful of us knows that help is available the moment we ask for it. Performance, or lack of it, has no effect on the giving of this Incurable Optimist.

In Benedict's monastery the novice is invited to climb the steps of humility. These reveal the true extent of the human 'shadow'. They show the extent of our pride, ambition, egotism, greed, power, possessiveness and the rest of it. By naming weakness, the novice grows in humility. This is not a virtue learnt from study; it is our response to the picture which comes ever more clear as we are accepted into the community. The secret gift is acceptance without having to pretend. Acceptance is the foundation for the love special in a monastic community. But we recall the words of a wise monk: 'We have to love the brethren, but we are not obliged to like them.'

In the Rule Benedict gives hope to those who falter as they climb the steps:

> After ascending all these steps of humility, the monk will quickly arrive at that perfect love of God, which casts out fear. Through this love, all that he once performed with fear, he will now begin to observe without effort, as though

naturally, from habit, no longer out of fear of hell, but out of love for Christ, good habit and delight in virtue.

Words like this encourage enthusiasm, but we have to be patient. The finale is unlikely to be achieved in this life. The perfect love of God, which has no fear, will only be really tasted in a life without end. For now we try to follow Benedict's exhortation: 'Let them prefer nothing whatever to Christ, and may he bring us all together to everlasting life.'

The rhythm, sameness and austerity of monastic life reveal vulnerability in a way nothing else does. Faced with failure, weakness and sin the only way forward is to put total trust in the Lord. 'Uphold me according to your promise, that I may live, and let me not be put to shame in my hope.' Words now with a new meaning.

It takes time, a long time. That is why, alongside the strong family life, there is plenty of sin, weakness and failure in monastic communities. Initial romanticism is replaced by something different, a combination of realism and enthusiasm. As we get nearer the light, the more confident we become. The promise of love in the future overpowers the dreariness of the present.

'Uphold me according to your promise, that I may live, and let me not be put to shame in my hope.' In making that cry, I know the Lord, the World's Most Incurable Optimist, is there to respond.

The Psalms deal not with types, but with individuals, and so there is inconsistency and variety just as there is in everyday human life. We are up one day and down the next; at one time sin seems a terribly black thing, at another it is simply 'missing the mark'; sometimes we love the whole world and there is no limit to our charity, at other times we cherish our own hearths and view everything and everybody outside them as aliens . . . At times we stand in awe of the eternal majesty of God – a thousand years in thy sight are but as yesterday – and at other times we are concerned only with this world and the future of people on this earth. Hence the Psalms tell us a great deal about human nature and they not only record experience, but they in turn have created experience in other people.

A. Victor Murray

People take account of our failure, but God of our striving.

Elizabeth Gibson

. . . The basic link between true living and order is God, the Life-Giver. He was active in creation. He bears forward and sustains the world, and all things are to be gathered up in his Christ. He drops his still dews and ordered lives, whether of individuals, nations, or churches, proclaim his peace, for he also can order 'unruly wills and affections'.

H. F. Woodhouse

I am sure God must have a sense of humour. I don't know how he could otherwise endure the creatures he has made.

Annie S. Swan

There is no tragedy so painful as the tragedy of a closed door – an unreceptive mind, an unresponsive soul. The divine Spirit waits to enter, and in his hand are such measures of happiness as we have never dreamed it possible for us to possess. Our true life, the beginning of our redeemed and everlasting life, must also wait, until we rise and open that door.

Anonymous

Take, Lord,
and receive all my liberty,
my memory, my understanding
and my entire will,
all that I have and possess.

You have given all to me;
to you, Lord, I return it.

All is yours;
do with it what you will.

Give me only your love
and your grace;
that is enough for me.

Ignatius

Brother,
you want to seek God with all your life,
and love him with all your heart.

But you would be wrong
if you thought you could reach him.
Your arms are too short, your eyes are too dim,
your heart and understanding too small.

To seek God
means first of all
to let yourself be found by him.
He is the God of Abraham, Isaac and Jacob.
He is the God of Jesus Christ.
He is your God,
not because he is yours
but because you are his.

To choose God
is to realise that you are known and loved
in a way surpassing anything men can imagine,
loved before anyone had thought of you
or spoken your name.

To choose God
means giving yourself up to him in faith.
Let your life be built on this faith
as on an invisible foundation.
Let yourself be carried by this faith
like a child in its mother's womb.

And so,
don't talk too much about God
But live
in the certainty that he has written your name
on the palm of his hand.
Live your human task
in the liberating certainty
that nothing in the world can separate you
from God's love for you.

From Rule for a New Brother

The courage to be myself eludes me,
A shadow of what might be I remain,
And all the while in other lives I see
The wholeness that I lack and can't attain.

The freedom to be myself eludes me,
For freedom itself does not liberate;
To be free to serve is the key to love
That can make of life a meaningful state.

The challenge of loving faith includes me,
I hear this call and can never stay out,
For love without faith is but sentiment
And faith is the courage to live in doubt.

>	E. M., a Nun of Burnham Abbey

There is not a heart but has its moments of longing, yearning for something better, nobler, holier than it knows now.

>	Henry Ward Beecher

Christianity is not believing the impossible, but doing the incredible.

>	*Sherwood Eddy*

When someone tells me he has never had a moment of probing religious doubt I find myself wondering whether he had ever known a moment of religious conviction.

>	Harold Bosley

*My Father, I abandon myself to you. Do with me as
 you will.
Whatever you may do with me, I thank you.
I am prepared for anything, I accept everything.
Provided your will is fulfilled in me and in all
creatures I ask for nothing more, my God.
I place my soul in your hands.
I give it to you, my God,
with all the love of my heart
because I love you.
And for me it is a necessity of love, this gift of myself,
this placing of myself in your hands
without reserve
in boundless confidence
because you are my Father.*

Charles de Foucauld

When God has told you what you ought to do, he has already told you what you can do.

W. S. Landor

God goes forward in his own ways, and proceeds as he began, in mercy. One of the most convenient hieroglyphics of God is a circle, and a circle is endless. Whom God loves he loves to the end; and not only to their own end, to their death, but to his end; and his end is, that he might love them still.

John Donne

. . . a faithful and generous God

Esther de Waal

Confidence and thanksgiving for God's purposes at work in the world run through Psalm 92 like threads in a tapestry, and it helps us to see God at work in his world and to respond with gratitude. Its opening line is a tremendous shout of praise, a great exclamation: 'It is good to give thanks . . .' In the terrible weeks that followed the events of 11th September 2001 in America, the *New Yorker* printed a poem which had at its heart this same theme: the importance of praise, of trying to praise, the necessity of praise even in a world which is suffering and bewildered. It was a translation by a Polish poet, Adam Zagajewski, and its opening words were: 'Try to praise the mutilated world . . .' Later the poet said, 'You must praise . . .' and then 'You should praise . . .' until by the end his refrain had become the simple exhortation 'Praise the mutilated world . . .' When I read it I felt that it had the same quality as the Psalms – which is seen nowhere more strongly than in this psalm – of the insistence on the role of praise, and of making an act of thanksgiving even when life is at its most painful and the world seems to be cruelly wounded and mutilated.

The Psalter is the prayer book of all Jewish and Christian people, and it is glorious to think of those who have sung and prayed these words and found strength and consolation in them in their very differing times and circumstances. 'For you, O Lord, have made me glad by your work' were words that Dante put into the mouth of the beatified souls in his *Paradiso*. In every age the works of God have been the reason for rejoicing – if only we can see his hand at work, even when we do not either recognise or understand his design. God rules, even when we seem to be surrounded by evil! 'But you, O Lord, are on high for ever' is the pivotal verse. There is such trust and confidence here. We acclaim that God's works are great and his designs are deep. For ultimately this psalm is a statement about the righteous ordering of human society, an affirmation of the sovereignty of God and of the deliverance of God's people.

It is interesting to find that scholars debate over the translation of vv10-11, asking whether this is the past or the future. Are the enemies defeated or is that still to come? It is probably best not to think of any particular deliverance which is a historic event but of the promise and certainty of that deliverance outside of time and to trust in the right ordering of the universe, and the scattering of whatever would destroy or threaten God's deep design.

Trusting in God is life-giving. God reveals himself both in creation and in his actions in the events of history, and not least in the events and circumstances of my life – if I interpret them aright. But so often I am foolish, a dullard, and then I fail to see, whether literally or metaphorically. Or if I translate the words of v6 as 'senseless' then it reminds me of the fullness of all my God-given senses to see, hear, feel, the right ordering of God at work around me.

I have found it helpful to read this psalm in the context of Psalm 1 which establishes so clearly the keynote theme which will run throughout the rest of the Psalter. It is an inescapable question for all of us: how are we to understand the conflict of good and evil? We see around us the righteous and the sinners and it often seems that the latter are springing up everywhere and are thriving. What is the issue about here? Sinners choose the wrong way; they refuse to be disciples, to listen to the word. The happy person is the person who delights in the law of the Lord – a law which is not a rigid legalism but a posture of constant openness, not a burden, but a delight! When I am open to God's word I am like a tree planted by the water for I am never without that river of life to sustain me.

This speaks of my dependency on a God who sustains and nurtures me. My perception of the world must be God-centred and not self-centred, and that is increasingly counter-cultural in a Western society which encourages an ideal of self-fulfilment and self-sufficiency. I am not too proud to say that I need help, that I have, in Calvin's happy phrase, 'a teachable frame', open to the many and various ways in which God will continually reveal himself in the world.

My own certainty and my strength come because I can depend on the steadfast love and faithfulness of God. God's truth and his love (v3) are there, by day and by night, and into my old age. I love the imagery of a tree. I am planted, firmly planted, with the root in its proper place, and it is this, of course, which allows for fruitfulness – a fulfilled and creative life which brings forth its proper fruits in due season. And this will go on even into old age, and I will continue to flourish. For those of us in the second half of life it is so good to find the psalmist referring to old age in such happy and positive terms. There is such a triumphant sense of confidence in the thought that we will still be full of sap, still green, not dried up and shrivelled as we get older.

The imagery of the psalms is so rich. Those who do not follow God and rely on his word will be like the grass which springs up but does not last long. But the trees that this speaks of are such a contrast! A palm tree, as anyone knows who has seen it in its native lands, is one of the most stately and graceful sights as it rises up proudly from often desert or stony ground. But it is more than that; it is a tree which is vitally useful, its fruits a staple diet for many people, its leaves made into baskets, its wood used as firewood. Even the thread of the web serves a purpose in rope-making. And then there is the further symbolic significance of palm leaves as a symbol of victory, twisted into a crown for the victor's brow, and of the branches used for celebration. The cedar is also one of the most glorious of all the trees. Growing up to a height of 40 feet and living to be thousands of years old, it is not surprising that it is often called the king of trees, an image of greatness and power.

The final image which the psalmist gives us at the very end is that of the rock. I pray that my life may be built not on shifting sands, but on a rock – and that rock is Christ. But as with all images there are so many levels of meaning. The rock stands for a secure foundation – 'He set my feet upon a rock' – but there is more, as the people of Israel found in their times of need in their desert wanderings. Water flows from the rock and the rock brings forth honey. There is sustenance as well as stability.

Why are the psalms so full of vitality? Why, if I say them aloud or better still sing them as part of my private prayer, do I find them so energising? Because they encourage me to live life to its fullest? I think that there is one very simple answer. The psalms place God at the centre of existence. Then everything else falls into its proper place. God is the giver of life, the creator of the divine order of the universe; God acts in history and in daily life. This God is a faithful and generous God and when I recall this I find that I want to celebrate, to proclaim aloud with a shout of praise and thanksgiving his loving faithfulness and steadfastness, which is there morning and night and until the end of my life.

We treat God with irreverence by banishing him from our thoughts, not by referring to his will on slight occasions. His is not the finite authority or intelligence which cannot be troubled with small things.

John Ruskin

I feel that a person may be happy in this world and I know that this world is a world of imagination and vision. I see everything I paint in this world, but everybody does not see alike. To the eye of the miser, a guinea is far more beautiful than the sun, and a bag worn with the use of money has more beautiful proportions than a vine filled with grapes. The tree which moves some to tears of joy is, in the eyes of others, only a green thing which stands in the way. As a man is, so he sees.

William Blake

It is as we go into the silence and quietly wait upon God that our little lives are taken up into the rhythms of the universe and given poise and peace.

G. T. Bellhouse

Let me learn the quiet of the evergreens,
The resilience of the robin and the starling in winter,
The concentration of snowdrops, crocus or daffodil.
Take me out of myself, that cupboard that needs spring-cleaning,
And let me remember the size of the moon and search the sky for it.
Count the cluster of stars, enjoy the rain's animation,
The energy of nature; let me now and then learn to be peaceful
And add a quiet to creation.

Elizabeth Jennings

God is a light that is never darkened, an unwearied life that cannot die, a fountain always flowing, a garden of life, a seminary of wisdom, a radical beginning of all goodness.

Francis Quarles

Nature is the living, visible, garment of God.

Goethe

The spring's warm breath . . . a sudden whisper in the summer leaves, the bird's clear song at early morning, will bring our souls into contact with the illimitable, telling us that we are one with ourselves, with Nature, and with God.

Dora Greenwell

The lasting wonder [of the Psalms] is that the psalmists ever rise to heights of beauty and devotion. Theirs is such a sense of the reality of God. The beauty of earth, stars, and the all-beholding sun is in their songs; the cry of the fugitive hunted for his life, the leper cast off from his people . . . the deep secret pangs of remorse, humiliation, repentance, and the joys of forgiveness . . . Their very phrases work their way into our hearts until we cannot let them go: 'the waters of comfort', 'the wings of the morning' 'the strength of the hills', 'the haven where they would be', 'the valley of the shadow of death'. . . Where, in all literature, is such a cross-section of human living in so small a space? On wings of song the Psalms come to us today as freshly and beautifully as to those who first heard them long ago.

Rita F. Snowden

If you say that God is good, great, blessed, wise or any such thing, the starting point is this: God is.

St. Bernard

O God, who broughtest me from the rest of last night
Unto the joyous light of this day,
Be thou bringing me from the new light of this day
Unto the guiding light of eternity.
Oh! From the new light of this day
Unto the guiding light of eternity.

          Carmina Gadelica

Where there is peace, God is.

          George Herbert

> Prayer is the peace of the spirit, the stillness of our thoughts, the evenness of our recollection, the sea of our meditation, the rest of our cares, the calm of our tempest.
>
>   Jeremy Taylor

I haste no more;
At dawn or when the day is done,
The sun comes calmly to his place,
I've learned the lesson of the sun.

I haste no more;
For spring or autumn, earth decrees,
The leaves shall bud, the leaves shall fall,
I've learned the lesson of the trees.

I haste no more,
At flood or ebb as it may be,
The ocean answers to the moon,
I've learned the lesson of the sea.

I haste no more;
Whate'er, who'er is mine,
These must, in God's ways, meet me in God's time,
I've learned the lesson, and I trust.

Anonymous

The serene, silent beauty of a holy life is the most powerful influence in the world, next to the might and spirit of God.

Blaise Pascal

Trusting in him who can go with me and remain with you, and be everywhere for good, let us confidently hope that all will be yet well.

Abraham Lincoln

... my refuge

Angela Griffiths

All who read the psalms will know that they have a unique way of speaking to the heart. Christ himself loved and prayed the Psalms. My own special favourite is Psalm 91. At one of the lowest points in my life God used words from this psalm to help me in a most unexpected way.

At the time I was a patient in a large city hospital a long way from home. I was in severe pain with a back injury, and had been taken on a trolley from the Orthopaedic Ward to another department, the Pain Clinic, where I was to have an injection in my spine. While I waited alone in one of the clinic cubicles, I stared up at the ceiling and fought back tears. I felt depressed, dejected, and exhausted from lack of sleep. Worst of all, I felt abandoned by God.

A doctor arrived with a nurse and a medical student. The doctor explained to me that the injection process was an intricate one, and therefore it was important that I keep very still.

While the injection was prepared I prayed inwardly. Then, to my surprise, I had a sudden, strong impression of divine wings above me. At the same moment, some words from Scripture jumped into my head:

> He will cover you with his pinions,
> and under his wings you will find refuge;
> his faithfulness is a shield and buckler.

I recognised the words as part of Scripture, but I had no idea which part. It was all so astonishing that I hardly noticed the next few minutes when the injection process began. All anxiety had left me, and in its place was an overwhelming feeling of peace and the assurance that God was with me, controlling everything.

Back in the ward some hours later, I thought over and over again about what had happened. But I could not explain such an intense spiritual experience. I knew it hadn't been caused by side-effects of the injection because it happened before the injection. It was possible that the Scripture text could have been in my memory from a past time. But what about the clear impression of wings over me? I did not think this had been just imagination. There is a discernible difference between things that are imagined and things that are of God.

I spent the next few hours trying to puzzle things out. When my daughter, Loveday, visited me after work that day, I told her what had happened. She has a strong, uncomplicated Christian faith. She thought the most likely explanation was that an angel of the Lord had been sent to help me.

After that I stopped trying to analyse events and just accepted the facts: God had blessed me in an unusual but very real way, and I was deeply thankful. In the days that followed I was still in considerable pain, but I no longer felt cut off from God. On the contrary, I felt that God was giving me new strength and with the new strength came a new frame of mind. I was filled with joy and passionate gratitude. Joy for all the miracles of life around me; gratitude for the help of hospital staff, for the cards and letters from friends with promises of prayer, for the smile of a stranger, even for the chirpy sparrows outside the ward window.

Being confined to bed, on traction, allows plenty of time for reflection. I wondered whether it was my lack of faith that had made God seem so remote lately. Then I recalled the events of Calvary when Jesus Christ cried out on the cross, 'My God, my God, why have you forsaken me?' This made me feel very close to Jesus, especially when I thought of his dying words, 'Father, into thy hands I commit my spirit.'

This was a turning point. I made a new commitment to God, and when I said, 'Thy will be done', it was a sincere prayer. I knew my brokenness, and my need for God's mercy and grace. It was a time for listening and learning and growing.

One of the things I realised was that for months, even years, I had been far too busy for my own spiritual good. The busyness had seemed quite valid at the time because much of it was concerned with church work. But now, I could see that I had allowed hectic activity to take the place of devotion. I had lost the habit of being still with God. In my zeal I had run ahead of God, instead of letting God lead. Prayer times had become rushed and there never seemed to be enough time for Bible reading. Somehow I had missed the clear example set by Jesus. His whole ministry was spent doing God's will, yet he was never overwrought. He knew the importance of regularly withdrawing from the crowds to have quiet communion with his Father, the source of his power.

During this time of enforced stillness I thought about the countless ways that God uses to communicate with us. I came to the conclusion that we can expect the unexpected, and if we are not ready to listen we risk not hearing. This means that patience is needed. I had not been patient. In all my months of over-activity I had just assumed I was going in the right direction. But acting without God's guidance means acting alone. Christ is the vine, we are the branches. We need to stay connected to Christ, to abide in Christ, if we are to be of use as modern-day disciples. Whether we are in full-time public ministry or called to the support work of visiting, befriending and encouraging, we all need to pray for one another. We can pray for those we know, and for those we don't know. As members of the body of Christ we need prayer to sustain us.

It was a teaching hospital I was in, so the daily routine was busy. But not a day went by when I did not think about the Scripture text that had come to me at the Pain Clinic. I had searched through the Gideon Bible in my bedside locker, but to no avail. However, the time was not wasted. What started out as a quest for one text in the Old Testament soon turned into a treasure trail through the pages of the New Testament. I rediscovered such lovely verses as 'My grace is sufficient for you, for my power is made perfect in weakness' (2 Corinthians 12:9) and 'We know that all things work together for good with those who love God, who are called according to his purpose' (Romans 8:28). These, and other verses, and the stories I read about Christ's ministry to real people in real situations gave me added strength.

At last the time came when I could leave hospital. I could only walk with the aid of crutches, but at least I was upright and relatively independent again. Soon after arriving home I used my Bible concordance and found the elusive words I had been searching for. They were part of Psalm 91. I read the psalm several times over and found it to be a powerful testimony of trust and praise. Again, I felt full of gratitude for the way that God had used words from this psalm to quicken new life in me.

In the months that followed there was further physical healing for my body, but more importantly there was a lot of spiritual regeneration going on. I learned more about waiting and receiving, and the value of stillness and silence. After a while God led me into new paths of service. This time I was careful not to rush ahead; instead I allowed God's power to work through me. Now, I am on a walk of faith rather than in a race, and I keep in step with my Companion.

There is no doubt that suffering is a dark experience. But out of our own pain can come a deep sense of empathy and compassion which can enable us to help ease the pain of others. In this fast-changing world none of us knows what a day will bring. But we can take comfort that we are not alone. The Lord, the Most High, our protecting Presence, is with us. And his angels are near, whether we are aware of them or not.

He calms the storms without and within, so that there can be trust and peace in the heart. Nothing can separate us from his love. With this faith and trust in my heart I can say, 'Though I am sometimes afraid, yet I will put my trust in you.' In all that happens we can be more than conquerors, we can win the victory over every fear, over every disturbance of mind, every worry, every hurt feeling. So like Jesus in the storm we can sleep in peace, saying and believing with the Psalmist: 'I will lie down in peace and take my rest, for it is thou, Lord, who makes me dwell in safety' (Psalm 4:7).

George Appleton

Let us give thanks unto the doer of good, and the merciful God,
the Father of our Lord, and our God and Saviour Jesus Christ:
for he hath sheltered us
he hath succoured us
he hath kept us
he hath redeemed us unto himself
he hath spared us
he hath helped us
he hath brought us to this hour.
Let us, therefore, pray to him
that he keep us in this holy day
and all the days of our life
in all peace, the almighty Lord our God.

Coptic Liturgy

In the silence of the night, all our roles and pretences slip away, leaving us vulnerable and alone. Occasionally tears, regrets or anxieties can creep into our beds as we lie awake trying to see through a jumble of loneliness, confusion or shame.

The psalms give us a language for such times of anguish and for the grace that shines through them. It is precisely in these moments of weakness or worry that God's life-giving presence upholds us and gives us hope. In the darkest nights of our soul's need, God can turn our tears into joy.

I think of you on my bed, and meditate on you in the watches of the night,' says Psalm 63:6. As we lie awake in the dark with all masks stripped away, God's sheer grace upholds us. Like a new-born clutching its mother, we cling for life to God's love for us, as we are, no matter what our failures or faults.

'You have been my help. In the shadow of your wings I sing for joy!' As shade is welcome in an arid land, so do we find the shadow of God's presence in our self-scorched souls (Psalm 121:5). As a hen gathers helpless chicks under her wings for protection and comfort, so God seeks to gather us (Matthew 23:37).

'My soul clings to you,' we cry out in the middle of our own deepest nights. And we sing, 'Your right hand upholds me!' In our sleepless times of mortality and unknowing, the uncertainty or woundedness in our lives causes us to admit our creatureliness. It is in such a 'dark night of the soul' that God's loving presence enfolds us, and we can sing for joy.

Betsy Schwarzentraub

That man is perfect in faith who can come to God in the utter dearth of his feelings and desires, without a glow or an aspiration, with the weight of low thoughts, failures, neglects and wandering forgetfulness, and say to him: 'Thou art my refuge.'

George Macdonald

. . . We find in the Bible the promises of God – 'Surely I will be with thee. I will never leave thee nor forsake thee. The Lord thy God shall be with thee, wherever thou goest' – given again and again to his servants, to assure them of the help and assistance of God in all their work for him. This assurance of God's continual help brings a peace to the soul not otherwise obtainable.

P. F. Holland

Learn to seek God and pray to him regularly during those quiet, mundane times of your life, trusting in his great and infinite loving mercy. Then, when life's storms blow over and around you threatening to engulf you in their ferocity, you can concentrate on what really matters, trusting in your heavenly Father to guide you safely through.

Source unknown

Deep and silent and cool as a broad, still tree-shaded river
Is the peace of thy presence, thou rest of our souls.
From the thousand problems of this our hurrying life
We turn, with silent joy, to plunge in thee,
To steep our souls in thy quiet depths
Where no clamour of earth disturbs our perfect content.
Thou art our home and refuge;
In thee we are safe and at peace:
Even in the din and hurry of the world
We know that thou art near,
We know that close at hand – closer than our little life –
Floweth that silent river of thy presence and love.
In a moment we may be with thee and in thee,
In a moment be surrounded and soaked in thy peace:
In a moment, as this loud world clangs round us,
We may rest secure in the bliss of thine eternity.

John S. Hoyland

God develops spiritual power in our lives through pressure of hard places.

Anonymous

I know
that when the stress has grown too strong,
thou wilt be there.
I know
that when the waiting seems so long,
thou hearest prayer.
I know
that through the crash of falling worlds,
thou holdest me.
I know that life and death are thine
eternally.

Janet Stuart

Earth has no sorrow that heaven cannot heal.

Thomas Moore

O Lord God, without whose will a sparrow doth not fall to the ground: grant us in all trouble and adversity to be quiet, without impatience and without murmuring, with our whole trust and confidence in thee, who workest all things for the best; to whom be glory for ever and ever.

Prayers of 1550

... Lord of lords and King of kings

Glennys Bamford

In my early teens my family moved to a new house, in a new area, which meant that we went to a new church. On the first Sunday morning there, I was amazed and nonplussed to discover what was then for me a strange practice. In place of the second hymn the congregation chanted a psalm from the back of the hymn book. It took me a long time to become familiar with how these were chanted, but eventually, as is usually the case with practise, it all became well-known and almost second nature. It meant that as a congregation we became familiar with psalms.

At first, the major problem with them was managing to sing them properly, or at least satisfactorily, so that I didn't stand out like a sore thumb. Eventually I even joined the choir, and was put with the contraltos – not a happy time. I have very little voice, and a very poor ear, and so was more of a liability than an asset. However, it meant that not only did I have to chant the psalm once on a Sunday, but practise it in choir practice. That meant that I began to look at the words. The psalms have a great multiplicity of themes, moods and attitudes. They were perplexing. Many reflected emotions, feelings, one's own situation. They reflected personal experience of God's sustaining presence. They were prayers for help, and of confession. However, so many more made me angry with talk of the destruction of sinners, and the awful fate awaiting Israel's enemies. That remains true of the Book of Psalms; some speak to one's deepest need, and express wonderfully one's experience of the grace of God. At different times, in different situations, different psalms are the ones one turns to. Psalm 23 is very important to me, as to almost all Christians, as a source of comfort, consolation, and the presence of God and his grace throughout our lives. Psalm 51 is the perfect expression of penitence, Psalm 139 of the sense that God is inescapable and knows all about us. And so one could go on. There is almost a psalm that fits one's mood on every occasion.

However, my experience of chanting in church included not only the psalms but the great hymns of the early church, and I have felt immensely privileged to have belonged to a church that regularly used in its worship the Benedictus, the Magnificat, the Nunc Dimittis and, above all, the Te Deum. The Te Deum became for me a very precious resource of praise and worship, and of very great personal significance and experience. In church, we sang it always on the first Sunday morning of the month, so it became very familiar. Of course, it is not strictly a psalm, but I hope it may count as one as, for me, it is always bound up with them.

The version I am most familiar with is that in the *Methodist Hymn Book*, and I find its language more meaningful than that in *Hymns & Psalms*. I hate to admit this, as I have always rejoiced in modern translations, and found it difficult to understand those who preferred the Authorised Version of the Bible. There has always been a peculiar excitement when there has been a new translation of the Bible produced by a panel of scholars, which sheds new light on familiar passages, and leads to new understanding. However, when I turned to the Te Deum in *Hymns & Psalms,* at last I understood why there are those who prefer the AV, though I'm sure we are right to update our translations and language. (I have persevered with the version in *Hymns & Psalms!*)

What is it that is so special to me about the Te Deum?

Probably the first thing about it is its history. It expresses the worship and faith of the Christian church through so many centuries. It gives continuity to our worship, and links us with Christians of many traditions, just as the ancient creeds do. This is important in faith, experience and worship. We need to do this in a living tradition, that includes our heritage, our contemporary contributions to faith and worship, so that our living tradition is passed on in a continuing stream.

Then it has great majesty. It expresses adoration. One cannot read or sing the Te Deum without being made aware of the greatness and majesty of God. We are not always very good at adoration in Methodist services. As I read or sing the Te Deum, I am filled with awe, and with the sense of being in the presence of the Lord of lords and King of kings. Added to that is the sense of all God's worshipping people, on earth and in heaven. I find it helpful to read and ponder before worship, and during a Communion service. It enables me to see myself in perspective, in the presence of God, and begin where I should begin, not with my concerns, but with the greatness and holiness of God.

It expresses our faith in Christ. It expresses Christ's work of redemption. It expresses the faith of the church as the creeds do. Yet it expresses that faith, and work of redemption, in a way that directly affects *me*. It says:
> We believe that thou shalt come to be our judge: we therefore pray thee, help thy servants, whom thou hast redeemed with thy precious blood.

That sends shivers through me. It expresses a true fear of the judgement of God, but always with our faith in the mercy of God, his loving kindness that forgives and heals. It saves us from over-familiarity, and our seeking for cheap grace, rather than the costly grace which is the gift of the gospel.

It is the last part, however, that most fully expresses our petition to God. It seeks salvation and guidance. We offer our worship and service, and ask God to sustain us and keep us.

> Vouchsafe, O Lord, to keep us this day without sin;
> O Lord, have mercy upon us, have mercy upon us.
> O Lord, let thy mercy lighten upon us as our trust is
> in thee: O Lord, in thee have I trusted, let me never
> be confounded.

In that is my prayer to God, seeking his grace and mercy, looking for strength to live as his disciple, and committing all that I have and am to him, in the assurance that he will hold me.

So the Te Deum moves from the glory of God, to my needs and his grace, and in that is the full spectrum of Christian worship and experience.

However, it is very special to me not only for its theology and its place in my personal history, but also because my father loved it. He was a Methodist, but with a strong Anglican background. He loved liturgy, and he had a strong sense of the holiness of God. The Te Deum was very important to him. He had a lovely rich tenor voice, and singing was his passion. He sang the Te Deum, and it expressed his faith. He said that above all else he wanted it sung at his funeral. We did. The choir came to lead the singing, and we all sang it for him, to express his faith in God, and to express ours. It was magnificent.

I can never again sing or say: 'O Lord, in thee have I trusted, let me never be confounded' without thinking of him, and his faith, and trusting myself to the same God. It expresses the faith of the whole church, militant and triumphant. As I read or sing it, I am aware of the God whom I worship, who created me, redeemed me and sustains me, and of my place among the great host through all generations who are the People of God.

All shall extol thee, thou Creator of all:
  O God,
Who openest every day the doors of the gates of the East,
And cleavest the windows of the firmament,
Bringing forth the sun from his place,
And the moon from her dwelling:
Giving light to the whole world and the inhabitants thereof,
Whom thou createdst by the attribute of mercy.

In mercy thou givest light to the earth
And to them that dwell thereon,
And in thy goodness renewest the creation every day
  continually.
O King, thou alone hast been exalted of yore,
Praised, glorified and extolled from days of old.

Jewish Prayer

Worship is not an instinct, it is a faculty. It is an instinct to satisfy our physical hunger by eating; and if we go without food for a long time we crave food. But it is not an instinct to satisfy our spiritual hunger by worship; and if we go without it for a long time, we do not crave worship. An instinct becomes more insistent and pressing the less it is satisfied; a faculty becomes less insistent and pressing the less it is satisfied. The more we exercise this faculty, the more we realise the need for it.

Thomas M. Morrow

Hosanna upon the earth . . . O Lord, vouchsafe blessings of fountains and the deep beneath, courses of sun, conjunctions of moons, summits of eastern mountains, of the everlasting hills.

Lancelot Andrewes

> The most wonderful thing we can experience is the mysterious, the sense of wonder about which something is partly known, partly hidden. The man to whom this emotion is a stranger, who can no longer stand rapt in awe and wonder is as good as dead.
>
> Albert Einstein

Thy whole creation speaks thy praise . . . that so our soul rises out of its mortal weariness unto thee, helped upward by the things thou hast made and passing beyond them unto thee who hast wonderfully made them: and there refreshment is and strength unfailing.

Augustine

Great and holy is the Lord,
  the holiest of holy ones for every generation.
Majesty precedes him,
  and following him is the rush of many waters.
Grace and truth surround his presence;
  truth and justice and righteousness are the foundation of his throne.
Separating light from deep darkness,
  by the knowledge of his mind he established the dawn.
When all his angels had witnessed it they sang aloud;
  for he showed them what they had not known;
Crowning the hills with fruit,
  good food for every living being.
Blessed be he who makes the earth by his power
  establishing the world in his wisdom.
In his understanding he stretched out the heavens,
  and brought forth the wind from his storehouses.
He made lightning for the rain,
  and caused mists to rise from the end of the earth.

Dead Sea Scrolls

Does not all nature around me praise God? If I were silent, I should be an exception to the universe. Does not the thunder praise him as it rolls like drums in the march of God of armies? Do not the mountains praise him when the woods upon their summits wave in adoration? Does not the lightning write his name in letters of fire? Has not the whole earth a voice? And shall I, can I, silent be?

Charles Spurgeon

To experience wonder is to utter an implicit prayer of thankfulness to the One whose majesty we have succeeded in glimpsing. Creation is inexhaustibly rich. At every level, the personal, the domestic, the natural, the cosmic, there are things to be discovered that will fill our hearts with joy and gladness. They will show us that we and all creation are fearfully and wonderfully made.

John Polkinghorne

There is a sublimity in little things. As the sun can be reflected by a dewdrop, so the whole infinitude of God's power and wisdom may shine up out of the arrangements which God has made for the comfort, progress, discipline and defence of his people.

Joseph Parker

Nothing must precede the worship of God.

St. Benedict

Thanks to thee, O God, that I have risen today,
   To the rising of this life itself;
May it be to thine own glory, O God of every gift,
   And to the glory of my soul likewise.

O great God, aid thou my soul
   With the aiding of thine own mercy;
Even as I clothe my body with wool,
   Cover thou my soul with the shadow of thy wing.

Help me to avoid every sin,
   And the source of every sin to forsake;
And as the mist scatters on the crest of the hills,
   May each ill haze clear from my soul, O God.

The Sun Dances, from the Gaelic

We are bidden to serve God not only with our heart and soul, but also with our mind, and that means that we should try and accustom ourselves to think of all truth and all beauty as showing us more of his character. We are far too ready to think of worship as being merely a matter of prayer, whereas really it should be a lifting up of our hearts in praise.

Cyril Allington

... the ultimate deliverer

Michael Nazir-Ali

I have chosen to write about Psalm 40 because it has been part of my devotional life for many years. The psalm consists of two contrasting parts: the first is a thanksgiving which praises God for deliverance from danger, disease and death. The second is a song of lament in which the writer asks God for deliverance from approaching dangers and enemies. Some feel that, for these reasons, the psalm must be a composite of two quite different poems. It is possible, however, to look at the matter in another way and to argue that the thanksgiving for past deliverance becomes the ground for hope as far as the future is concerned. In other words, the two parts are interconnected.

Down the ages, the psalm has appealed to a wide variety of people. The 1650 Scottish Psalter has a version which begins:

> I waited for the Lord my God,
> and patiently did bear;
> At length to me he did incline,
> my voice and cry to hear.

More recently the Iona Community has produced a version which can be sung to the tune of 'Amazing Grace':

> I waited patiently for God,
> for God to hear my pray'r;
> And God bent down to where I sank
> and listened to me there.

The contemporary song, 'Faithful One', also echoes some of the psalm's sentiments:
> You lift me up when I fall down;
> all through the storm your love is the anchor;
> my hope is in You alone.'

The form in which I have mostly used this psalm is in the Punjabi translation of the Revd Dr. Imam Din Shahbaz. The translation of the Psalms into Punjabi and their setting to popular folk-tunes has provided the Punjabi-speaking church in many parts of the world with a major resource for worship and devotion. Although the psalms were first translated for Presbyterians, they are now used by every part of the Christian community. Most recently, the Roman Catholic Church has made a notable contribution in having them recorded for mass distribution. In the past, Anglicans have adapted them for use in a more formal liturgical context.

For the churches in Pakistan and India, psalms of thanksgiving and of lament are very popular. Psalm 40 is liked particularly because it brings the two themes together and celebrates trust in God. I used to sing this psalm often with the bonded labourers with whom I was working in the brick-kilns. In spite of the church's efforts to improve their condition and even the beginnings of a movement of protest, their lot was such that God was, indeed, their only hope. I could only admire their patience! They would praise God for what little they had: lentils, onions and chapattis to eat, good weather so they could work, relative health for the strength needed in their back-breaking work, simple shelters for their children. They would then plead for God's help in their sickness, against oppressive employers, that their debts may be more manageable and that their children might be freed from bondage to an oppressive system.

In this psalm there is already a sense that God is the *ultimate* deliverer. He rescues us not just from our day-to-day troubles (he may do that) but he is the one who rescues us from the meaninglessness of death and non-existence itself. It is trust in God and the doing of his will which are of primary importance. The poet does not do away with the external signs of religion and its ritual but, as elsewhere in the Bible, assigns them a secondary place: prayers, songs and sacrifice are acceptable to God when they are an expression of trust and not otherwise (cf. 1 Samuel 15:22; Psalm 50:8-14; 51:16f; Hosea 6:6; Amos 5:21f; Micah 6:6-8).

God's mighty acts of redemption are not just experienced by his people but they have the task of proclaiming them far and wide. The Letter to the Hebrews identifies Jesus Christ as the truly blessed man who puts his trust in God and sets about doing his will, even to the point of rejection, suffering and death (Hebrews 10:5-10). We find our blessing in the following of Jesus and in his presence amongst us. We need to accept this blessing whilst acknowledging our poverty and need. These may be of a different order from those working in a brick-kiln in Pakistan but they are, nevertheless, just as real. Recognising our wretchedness is ever the first sign in the Bible of repentance, of throwing ourselves onto God's ever-present mercy and of trusting in his love to rescue us from 'the miry bog' into which we have got ourselves. God's steadfast love and faithfulness are the basis for our own faith in him.

Those who have been redeemed can sing the song of their redemption, as did Moses, Miriam and the people of Israel at the time of their rescue from slavery in Egypt (Exodus 15:1-21).

Of course, I sing this psalm with the company of God's people as we acknowledge our need for rescue and celebrate God's redemption, but I sing it to myself also when I need to calm myself, to be patient in the face of adversity and to prepare for declaring God's mighty acts in the midst of the congregation. The psalms, as a whole, and this one in particular, are such a huge spiritual resource for me and for many other Christians. Are they for you?

> No song, it was felt by the ancient Psalmist, could be too jubilant for a people who had in Jehovah one so wondrous in his fidelity and grace. Both for what he was in all his matchless attributes, and for all that he was ever doing in his acts of gracious providence and miraculous deliverances, they must ever shout for joy.
>
> W. E. Farndale

When I am out of heart, I follow David's example, and fly for refuge to prayer, and he furnishes me with a store of prayer.

I am bound to acknowledge I have always found that my prayers have been heard and answered . . . In almost every instance I have received what I have asked for. Hence I feel permitted to offer up my prayers for everything that concerns me. I am inclined to think there are no little things with God. His hand is as manifest in the feathers of a butterfly's wing, in the eye of an insect, in the folding and packing of a blossom, as in the creation of the world and in the laws by which planets move. I understand literally the injunction, 'In everything make your requests known unto God', and I cannot but notice how amply these prayers have been met.

T. Fowell Buxton

You are holy, Lord, the only God, and your deeds are wonderful.
You are strong, you are great.
You are the Most High, you are almighty.
You, Holy Father, are King of heaven and earth.
You are Three in One, Lord God, all good.
You are good, all good, supreme good, Lord, living and true.

You are love, you are wisdom.
You are humility, you are endurance.
You are rest, you are peace.
You are joy and gladness, you are justice and moderation.
You are all our riches, and you suffice for us.

You are beauty, you are gentleness.
You are our protector, you are our guardian and defender.
You are courage, you are our haven and our hope.

You are our faith, our great consolation.
You are our eternal life, great and wonderful Lord,
God almighty, merciful Saviour.

Francis of Assisi

No-one understands what love is in itself, but such are its workings, it giveth more than one can take, and asks more than one can pay.

Jan Ruysbroeck

If we do not find God in the events of history, it is because we have blinded ourselves to the manner of his approach to people; for he is in all history, in all true interpretation of history, and in the words of those who have caught some knowledge of the eternal purpose he is working out.

P. T. R. Kirk

Eternal Light, shine into our hearts,
Eternal Goodness, deliver us from evil,
Eternal Power, be our support,
Eternal Wisdom, scatter the darkness of our ignorance,
Eternal Pity, have mercy upon us;
    that with all our heart and mind and soul and strength
    we may seek thy face and be brought
    by thine infinite mercy to thy holy presence;
through Jesus Christ, our Lord.

Alcuin

Although God is so great and powerful, although the universe has its imagination-defying immensities, God is also the God of the least detail. To see a snowflake under the microscope is to see a detailed loveliness beyond the skill of man to create. The universe tells not only of the infinite greatness of God; it tells also of the infinite care of God of the smallest things.

William Barclay

Eternal God . . .
When the day seems dark before me,
Give me grace to walk trustingly:
When the distant scene is clouded, let me rejoice
that at least the next step is plain . . .
When insight falters, let obedience stand firm,
What I lack in faith, let me repay in love.

John Baillie

I took up the Bible and began to read; having opened the book casually, the first words that occurred to me were these, 'Call on me in the day of trouble, and I will deliver, and thou shalt glorify Me.' Before I lay down, I did what I never had done in all my life; I kneeled down and prayed to God to fulfil the promise to me, that if I called upon him in the day of trouble, he would deliver me.

Daniel Defoe

O God, the refuge of the poor, the strength of those who toil, and the Comforter of all who sorrow, we commend to your mercy the unfortunate and needy in whatever land they may be. You alone know the number and extent of their sufferings and trials. Look down, Father of mercies, at those unhappy families suffering from war and slaughter, from hunger and disease, and other severe trials. Spare them, O Lord, for it is truly a time for mercy.

St. Peter Canisius

> *God, we believe that you have called us together to broaden our experience of you and of each other. We believe that we have been called to help in healing the wounds of society and in reconciling people to each other and to God. Help us, as individuals or together, to work, in love, for peace, and never to lose heart. We commit ourselves to each other – in joy and sorrow. We commit ourselves to all who share our belief in reconciliation – to support and stand by them. We commit ourselves to the way of peace – in thought and deed. We commit ourselves to you – as our guide and friend.*
>
> *Corrymeela Community Prayer*

When speaking of divine perfection, we signify that God is just and true and loving, the author of order, not disorder, of good, not evil. We signify that he is justice, that he is truth, that he is love, that he is order, that he is the very progress of which we were speaking, and that wherever these qualities exist, whether in the human soul or in the order of nature, there God exists. We might still see him everywhere, if we had not been mistakenly seeking for him apart from us, instead of in us; away from the laws of nature instead of in them. And we become united, not by mystical absorption, but by partaking of that truth and justice and love which he himself is.

Plato

... closer than breathing

Rachel Newton

Going to the cinema recently I was surprised to hear a quotation from the Psalms. It was in the film *Iris*, made from the book by John Bailey, married to the philosopher and writer Iris Murdoch. John Bailey wrote about his courtship, marriage and his wife's decline into Alzheimer's disease before her death. It is a moving book, naïve in places but touching and infinitely tender, prompting one to reflect as in Shakespeare's *Hamlet*, 'Oh, what a noble mind is here o'erthrown.' The book translated well into a film, with the younger Iris played by Kate Winslet and the older by Judi Dench.

Iris, who had been a striking-looking young woman, not conventionally beautiful but with a string of admirers, was also the talk of Oxford academia with her popular lectures and her successful and intriguing novels which made her famous worldwide. Iris had a deeply spiritual side but she was not a regular churchgoer and sometimes sat lightly to religion while observing and writing about religious people. Yet here she was, in one of her public lectures at the height of her powers, quoting from a favourite psalm.

Why should that surprise me? I suppose it says something about the secular age in which we live that I am surprised by a biblical reference or religious language in an everyday context. I am reminded of what Susanna Wesley said in her time, the 18th century, that 'the utmost care and diligence have been used to banish all discourse of God or spiritual concerns out of society, as if religion were never to appear out of the closet and we were to be ashamed of nothing so much as professing ourselves to be Christians'. She would warn us to be wary of closing our minds down to genuine exchange about matters which concern our souls. Yet we live in an age where there is a spiritual hunger and if we can talk easily and naturally about our beliefs who knows what might happen?

For a long time I think I took the Psalms for granted. Yes, I read them and sang them in worship, and the Anglican 'bit' of me enjoyed that. I was stunned, too, when I first heard them sung by a Jewish choir in a synagogue. I found the sound haunting and quite beautiful, with all the yearning of a people in exile. Then gradually I found that words from the Psalms came to me and began to speak personally, not just in the beautiful poetry.

My favourite is Psalm 139. It is one from which I cannot escape, and which when pondered on and prayed with, gives me an incredible sense of belonging in this world – my *raison d'être*, I would say.

This psalm is a hymn of praise to God, but is also incredibly personal – me speaking directly to my Maker and Creator. I feel as if it acknowledges the source of my being from the beginning of my time here on earth – indeed, before that – the knitting of me together in my mother's womb, the knowing of me through and through. My faults, my reticences, my growing: nothing has escaped attention, even in the smallest detail. All this is too wonderful for me. This is both a huge responsibility, coupled with a striving to be the best that I can be, but also with a sense of having a huge comfort blanket, which wraps me round and secures me to my roots.

I have the same tingling feeling whenever I read the first stanza of that marvellous narrative poem by Gerard Manley Hopkins, 'The Wreck of the Deutschland':

> Thou mastering me
> God! Giver of breath and bread;
> World's strand, sway of the sea,
> Lord of living and dead;
> Thou hast bound bones and veins in me,
> fastened me flesh,
> And after it almost unmade, what with dread,
> Thy doing: and dost thou touch me afresh?
> Over again I feel thy finger and find thee.

The awesome, mysterious God, the Creator, who is accessible and touchable, closer than breathing, is there for us.

I am reminded of the story of Adam and Eve in the various versions of the Mystery plays I have either seen or directed over the years, including the wonderful South African interpretation of the Chester Cycle in 2002. The two human figures being formed out of the sand of the earth emerge as innocent new-born adults full of wonder and delight – 'intricately woven in the depths of the earth' as v15 says. In this psalm I can go back to that innocence, though there have been many falls from grace in between.

Knowing oneself to be a beloved child of God creates a buffer against the world and a huge advantage in dealing with the difficulties of life. This is not smugness or one-upmanship, but reality.

In my career I dealt with some very damaged young people in society, who had ended up in special schools because their violence and poor behaviour had lead to exclusion. I was brought up sharply time and again to recognise that circumstances, poor relationships and abuse resulted in low self-esteem. If someone is constantly told that they are no good, a nuisance, in the way, battered at verbally and maybe physically, they begin to believe it. One boy, when he finally finished a piece of writing or art-work, would always tear it up. He never believed it was any good, no matter what anyone else said. Others would fight back aggressively and take it out on someone else, or spoil things that others did. There are so many ways of fighting back at what the world has done to you.

What a gulf between the privileged child of God who knows they are loved and the rejected who don't even know it, let alone believe it. Yet the assurance of the love of God, as demonstrated in the gospels through the person of Jesus, is open to all, not just for the privileged few, if only it can be communicated.

Another boy, grieving for his brother who had been killed when he crashed a stolen car, said to me, 'You believe in God, don't you, miss? I just hope he loves Paul, now that he's dead.' I hope the reply, 'Yes, and he loves you too' was some comfort to him.

In spite of all the evil and hurt in the world, the sadness and the failures, we are able, like the psalmist, to swell with the praise of the God who created the heavens, spangled the stars and formed the beauty of the butterfly, because this God also made me.

God, the creator, potter, risk-taker, one who is neither male nor female but the best of both; one full of mystery and surprise, beyond our expectation and imagining: I praise and adore you.

I thank thee, God, that I have lived
In this great world, and known its many joys;
The song of birds, the strong sweet scent of hay
And cooling breezes in the secret dusk,
The flaming sunsets at the close of day,
Hills, and the lonely, heather-covered moors,
Music at night, and moonlight on the sea,
The beat of waves upon the rocky shore
And wild, white spray, flung high in ecstasy:
The faithful eyes of dogs, and treasured books,
The love of kin and fellowship of friends,
And all that makes life dear and beautiful.
I thank thee, too, that there has come to me
A little sorrow and, sometimes, defeat,
A little heartache and the loneliness
That comes with parting, and the word, 'Goodbye',
Dawn breaking after dreary hours of pain,
When I discovered that night's gloom must yield
And morning light break through to me again.
Because of these and other blessings poured
Unasked upon my wondering head,
Because I know that there is yet to come
An even richer and more glorious life,
And most of all, because thine only Son
Once sacrificed life's loveliness for me –
I thank thee, Lord, that I have lived.

Elizabeth Craven

In the morning prayer is the key that opens to us the treasures of God's mercies and blessings; in the evening it is the key that shuts us up under his protection and safeguard.

Anonymous

Worship is the submission of all our nature to God. It is the quickening of conscience by his holiness; the nourishment of mind with his truth; the purifying of the imagination by his beauty; the opening of the heart to his love; the surrender of will to his purpose – and all of this gathered up in adoration, the most selfless emotion of which our nature is capable and therefore the chide remedy of that self-centredness which is our original sin and the source of all actual sin.

William Temple

> When beauty fires the blood,
> God's love fires the mind.
>
> *Dryden*

Gratitude is not only the memory but the homage of the heart rendered to God for his goodness.

N. P. Willis

Blessed are you, Lord our God, king of the universe. By his word he brings on the evening twilight; in wisdom he opens the gates of the dawn, and with foresight makes time pass and seasons change. He sets the stars in their courses in the sky according to his plan. He creates day and night, turning light into darkness and darkness into light. He makes the day fade away and brings on the night, and separates day and night, for he is the Lord of the hosts of heaven.

>Forms of Prayer for Jewish Worship

>How does God speak to us?
>He speaks to us through our past.
>He speaks to us in our present situation.
>And he speaks to us through our own arguments,
>through our fears and failures,
>through his love,
>through other people,
>books,
>pain and suffering.
>He speaks to us by every possible means
>At every possible time.

>>Rosalind Rinker

I am aware
As I go commonly sweeping the stair
Doing my part of the everyday care –
Humbly simple my lot and my share,
I am aware of a marvellous thing:
Voices that murmur and others that ring
In the far stellar spaces where cherubim sing.

I am aware of the passion that pours
Down the channels of fire through infinity's doors,
Forces terrific with melody shod,
Music that mates with the pulses of God;
I am aware of the glory that runs
From the core of myself to the core of the suns.

Bound to the earth by invisible chains,
Blaze of eternity now in my veins,
Seeing the rush of ethereal rains,
Here in the midst of this everyday air -
I am aware.

I am aware
As I sit quietly here in my chair -
Human and simple my lot and my share.
I am aware of the systems that swing
Through the isles of creation on heavenly wing.
I am aware of a marvellous thing:
Trail of the comets in furious flight,
Thunders of beauty that shatter the night,
Terrible triumph of pageants that march
To the trumpets of time through eternity's arch.

I am aware of the splendour that ties
All the things of the earth with the things of the skies;
Here in my body the heavenly heat –
Here in my flesh the melodious beat
Of the planets that circle Divinity's feet –
As I sit quietly here in my chair
I am aware.

                                        Angela Morgan

> *Some thoughts always find us young, and keep us so. Such a thought is the love of the universal and eternal beauty.*
>
>   *Ralph Waldo Emerson*

O God our Father, good beyond all good, blessed above all blessedness, and wise beyond all wisdom, remove the barriers that divide us from one another, and bring us into such unity in you that our lives may bear some likeness to your own.

                                        Dionysius (adapted)

... my inheritance

Tom Taylor

My expectations, as a child or an adolescent, were not great. I had no apparent gifts or talents, either artistic or academic. Nor was there an anticipated legacy from a wealthy benefactor, since I came from average working-class stock and was nurtured in the working environment of the 1920s and 30s. The possibility of moving away from this pattern of life never occurred to me. Like most of my contemporaries I finished my formal education at the age of 14 and took my place in industry, before I joined the army in 1939.

My prospects for advancement in any field appeared no better when in 1945, at the age of 22, I was almost fatally wounded whilst leading an infantry section in one of the bloodiest little battles of the Burma campaign. A Japanese sniper's bullet passed through my head and I was left for dead until I was discovered several days later by the battalion stretcher-bearers, and removed from the battlefield, naked, emaciated and a mere shell of a human being with the residue of congealed blood, pus and dirt clinging to my matted hair and unshaven beard. The gunshot wound had deprived me permanently of my eyesight, my senses of smell and taste. I gradually regained consciousness in the base hospital far removed from the combat zone after lingering for over two months between life and death. In the meantime some delicate brain surgery and other treatment had taken place. I thought at first that my injuries were only temporary, and that I would soon be rejoining my comrades at the front, but this was not to be. Coming back into the real world again, there were strong indications that my life chances were only slender and that drastic adjustments to my way of life would have to be made: thus, I faced a very uncertain future.

Nevertheless, in spite of my afflictions, I can say with the psalmist: 'The boundary lines have fallen for me in pleasant places; I have a goodly heritage' (Psalm 16:6). This passage focuses on one of the important themes of the Bible – birthright and inheritance. According to some commentators, Psalm 16 is a spiritual reflection of Joshua, and refers to the distribution of land and property bestowed on the extended family of Israel following their occupation of Cana under Joshua's leadership.

My own inheritance, though on a vastly smaller scale, is no less valuable to me. It consists of a few small items – a ring, a leather wallet, a tie-pin, an ornamental fish, a silver-plated Yale key, and a hand-made brass cross. My ex-serviceman's badge, and the commemorative crown coin which were given me, and my invitation from the Master of the Royal Household to meet the Queen in Buckingham Palace may also be included. None of these articles carry an expensive price tag, but they are priceless treasures to me.

The ring was given to me by the headman of a small Indian village in the Punjab, now part of Pakistan. The simple but generous gesture was made at the end of an overnight exercise which had involved a long tiring march under the scorching sun. The hospitality was frugal, but genuine. As we were leaving the village, the man took the ring, bearing a tiny ruby stone, off his finger with the words, 'Take this, sahib, and when you go home, think of us.' They are words which are indelibly printed on my mind, and I am unlikely ever to forget them. Unfortunately, less than one year later, this ring was removed from my finger by the Japanese soldiers who overran our position, in January 1945, along with everything else I was wearing whilst I lay critically wounded. But no one can erase the memory or destroy the relationship I feel that I have with that Indian family.

The wallet was made by a group of Indian Red Cross women working in the rehabilitation of wounded servicemen in a military hospital in South India during the very early stages of my convalescence. On my departure for the UK the wallet, embossed with the symbols of India, and also marked with my own signature, my first effort after my wounding, was presented to me.

The tie-pin belonged to my father, and he always wore it with his 'Sunday-best'. The pin is made from a half sovereign, and engraved with the full text of the Lord's Prayer. It can only be properly read with the aid of a magnifying glass. As it is gold, it never tarnishes. My mother gave it to me when my father died.

The fish was a surprise gift from a fellow patient just before I was invalided out of the army. This young soldier from Northern Ireland occupied the bed next to mine in an Oxford hospital. Eventually he showed me a beautifully crafted ornamental fish made of perspex, fitted with fins, and with a tiny coloured eye, cut from a toothbrush, all suitably fixed to a matching stand. Hours of painstaking labour must have been spent on this piece of work even before I met him. I presumed it was intended for someone special, and thought little more about it. When I moved on to take my final medical board, my hospital companion helped me pack my valise, and I did not know that he had planted the fish in a small parcel beneath my other belongings. I only discovered it weeks later when our paths had already taken different turnings. I always regret that there was no opportunity to express my full appreciation and thanks for this marvellous gesture.

The silver-plated key was presented to me by Rev Harold McKee, the minister of Bolton Road Methodist Church, Bury, after I had performed the opening ceremony of the Memorial Hall, which I had been asked to do as a former member of the Sunday school. The room is an annex to the church hall commemorating members of the church who were killed in the two world wars. The key symbolises the granting of the 'freedom' of the hall to me.

The solid brass cross stands about four inches high on three shallow plinths in the traditional style. It was made by the brother of the woman who gave it to me at the time when refugees from Europe were being invited to this country. The church I attended at the time made a great effort to support this cause, which received much commendable publicity. Unfortunately it also drew an irate response from a reader of the local newspaper, who sent a letter of complaint to the effect that more was being done for these incomers than was being done for people like her and her family, who were living in distressed circumstances. With permission a visit was made, and help given. It was then that the lady put the cross in my hand, saying, 'Have this, it may mean more to you than to me.'

These artefacts are a symbolic representation of my journey of faith.

A ring is a symbol of unity. We use it as a sign of commitment to a bonded relationship in the marriage ceremony. The Father of the Prodigal Son put a ring on the returned son's finger to signify his return home and to a restored relationship. I believe that the ring given to me marks a bond of friendship between that Asian family and me, established long ago.

Handling the wallet not only reminds me of the help I was given at a critical period of my life, but of what Jesus said to his disciples about not carrying a wallet on their missions, that adequate provision would always be made for them. This is something I have found to be true in my work for the kingdom.

My father's gold tie-pin containing the Lord's Prayer brings back a lifetime of memories of my dad, but of equal significance is the gift of God's written word, and the relationship we have with our Heavenly Father.

Keys are necessary instruments of security, giving access to secured or closed places. Theoretically, I need not ever lack a shelter whilst the Memorial Hall exists, because the key in my possession gives me access to this room.

The fish which I was given by my friend in hospital connects us all as servants and fellow-workers of God's kingdom, with the early disciples, with all who have laboured in the intervening years, and all those, too, who have been persecuted and suffered for their faith. Because of the maltreatment they experienced, the early disciples were compelled to meet in secret, identifying themselves and their locations by the sign of the fish. This remained the recognised symbol of the infant church until the period of Constantine in the fourth century.

The cross is more than a symbol to be handed down: it is a necessary part of the Christian's make-up. To quote the words of Jesus: 'If any want to become my followers, let them deny themselves and take up their cross and follow me' (Matthew 16:24). As a preacher I am reminded of what St. Paul said, 'For Christ did not send me to baptise but to proclaim the gospel . . . for the message of the cross is foolishness to those who are perishing, but to us who are being saved it is the power of God' (1 Corinthians 1:17-18). Every servant of the Lord is vitally dependent on this power to fulfil the tasks assigned to him. It has been the motivating force which has moved the church forward from age to age, even to the present day.

My personal invitation to attend a reception at Buckingham Palace in May 2001, and to have the experience of meeting the sovereign face-to-face and shaking her hand, is my most recent and memorable addition to my inheritance.

The badge I was given on my discharge from active service bears the royal emblems and the words, 'For Loyal Service'. Forty-eight years ago I was received onto 'Full Plan' as a fully-accredited Local Preacher. At the end of my days I trust that I may be awarded a similar accolade. I was given a crown to mark Queen Elizabeth II's Coronation in 1953, and I am not without hope that the cross I have inherited will be exchanged 'one day for a crown'. This is not presumption but a promise to be fulfilled.

Editor's Note: Tom Taylor died before he had fully completed this article. For his family and for all who knew him, there can be no doubt that the hope he expressed in his final paragraph has been fulfilled.

To you, Creator of nature and humanity, of truth and beauty, I pray:

Hear my voice, for it is the voice of the victims of all wars and violence among individuals and nations.

Hear my voice, for it is the voice of all children who suffer and will suffer when people put their faith in weapons and war.

Hear my voice when I beg you to instil into the hearts of all human beings the wisdom of peace, the strength of justice and the joy of fellowship.

Hear my voice, for I speak for the multitudes in every country and in every period of history who do not want war and are ready to walk the road of peace.

Hear my voice and grant insight and strength so that we may always respond to hatred with love, to injustice with total dedication to justice, to need with the sharing of self, to war with peace.

O God, hear my voice, and grant unto the world your everlasting peace.

Pope John Paul II, on a visit to Hiroshima

O God, we thank you for the
glorious opportunities
to build new societies
of peace, justice and love
to praise and glorify you.
Help us, we pray,
to stand up with courage,
to work with love
and to live in hope
for Christ's sake.

Unknown

The wonderful thing about the grace of God, of course, is that it is like the Spirit herself: it is no respecter of persons or of theological boundaries. Although I as a Catholic value the sacrament of reconciliation and find it a powerful visible sign of God's invisible grace, I do not for one moment think that God's grace be confined. The grace of God is like our child's conception of a raygun – it is invisible, all penetrating, defies all barriers. When I speak in this manner I am in no way denying my Christian heritage, merely acknowledging the greatness and inscrutability of the Divine.

Sheila Cassidy

When I am with God
My fear is gone
In the great quiet of God.
My troubles are as the pebbles on the road
My joys are like the everlasting hills.

Walter Rauschenbusch

> *God is with those who persevere.*
>
> *Anonymous*

Each of us may be sure that if God sends us on stony paths he will provide us with strong shoes. He will not send us out on any journey for which he does not equip us well.

Source unknown

His grace is great enough to meet the great things –
The crashing waves that overwhelm the soul,
The roaring winds that leave us stunned and breathless,
The sudden storms beyond our life's control.

His grace is great enough to meet the small things –
The little pin-prick troubles that annoy,
The insect worries, buzzing and persistent,
The squeaking wheels that grate upon our joy.

Annie Johnson Flint

My Father, in this dark, troubled time, help me to receive your gift of inward serenity. May I prove day by day that you will keep in perfect peace those whose minds are stayed on you.

Anonymous

Hope, child, tomorrow and tomorrow still,
And every tomorrow hope; trust while you live.
Hope, each time the dawn doth heaven fill
Be there to ask; God is there to give.

Victor Hugo

The good news is that while there may be circumstances over which God does not have absolute control and 'things' that God does not cause, there is *no* thing that God cannot turn to good. God may not be the author of all things, but God is the master of all things. There is no event, no experience of human life, that God cannot somehow weave into the tapestry of God's good purpose for us. There is no accident or incident of human life that cannot become grist for the mill of God's redemptive purpose in the world and in our experience. There is no thing that God cannot use in some way for good.

James A. Harnish

One thing stirs me when I look back at my youthful days: the fact that so many people gave me something or were something to me without knowing it . . . Much that I should otherwise not have felt so clearly or done so effectively was felt or done as it was, because I stand, as it were, under the sway of these people. Hence I always think that we live, spiritually, by what others have given to us in the significant hours of our life.

Albert Schweitzer

The gloom of the world is but a shadow. Behind it, yet within our reach, is joy. There is radiance and glory in the darkness, could we but see; and to see, we have only to look. I beseech you to look.

Life is so generous a giver, but we, judging its gifts by their covering, cast them away as ugly, or heavy or hard. Remove the covering and you will find beneath it a living splendour, woven of love, by wisdom, with power. Welcome it. Grasp it, and you touch the angel's hand that brings it to you. Everything we call a trial, a sorrow or a duty: believe me, that angel's hand is there; the gift is there; and the wonder of an overshadowing Presence.

Life is so full of meaning and of purpose, so full of beauty – beneath its covering – that you will find that the earth but cloaks your heaven. Courage, then, to claim it; that is all! But courage you have, and the knowledge that we are pilgrims together, wending through unknown country, home.

And so I greet you; with the prayer that for you, now and for ever, the day breaks and the shadows flee.

Father Giovanni, 1513

Let your love, O Lord, fall as fire from heaven upon the altars of our hearts. Strengthen thou our souls; awaken us, that we may no longer as in a dream, but walk before you as pilgrims in earnest to reach their home. And grant us all at last to meet before your throne, and there rejoice in your love.

Gerhard Tersteegen (adapted)

...my guide and Father

Andy Reed

At some stage of every day I have to pinch myself to believe that I am a Member of Parliament. I look to the past and how God has brought me to this place. I never set out to become an MP. People from my school were never really destined to become MPs or great civic leaders. If we were lucky there would be one person in each year deemed good enough to take an entrance exam for Oxford or Cambridge. Our aspirations were quite limited.

As I sat down to contemplate this article I realised one thing that was crying out very clearly and why I was so pleased to be able to contribute to the book. I have trusted God to do what he wants with my life, and the more faith I place in him the easier it becomes to trust. At times of tribulation, or indeed of decision-making about the direction my life should take, I have been aware of God's guiding hand.

I was a young lad with political thoughts. My political concerns and issues had grown out of our Methodist youth group. I suppose most youth groups played table-tennis – but we had discussions and debate. I clearly remember being moved by the plight of the starving in the third world juxtaposed with meat mountains and wine lakes in Europe. God could easily feed the world yet our greed and inability to distribute the food caused so much misery for millions. Our aid budget was pitiful and countries were paying back more in interest on their debt. There had to be a better way to run the world, I thought as an enthusiastic teenager. After a few letters to my MP I felt that there was more I could do. I studied the possibility of voluntary work overseas, but not being very practical I felt that this was not meant for me. I was angry, fired up about injustice, poverty and the misery it caused, yet I had no idea what to do.

There was no flash of light or a clear sign from God that I should become an MP. He doesn't seem to work that way with me. Before the 1992 General Election I had been 'promoted' within my constituency party to Chair, and had accidentally been elected to my local parish council. I found out later that, far from being given jobs because people thought I was so wonderful, they had been trying to get somebody else to do the donkey-work for a long time and nobody was daft enough to take it on. I walked in as the new boy and unsuspectingly agreed to every job they offered me. How this reminded me so much of my church!

I was elected to the Parish Council as a Labour councillor in a village totally dominated by the Conservatives when I was put forward as a paper candidate with a clear promise that there was no chance of winning. Unfortunately the local Conservatives were a bit disorganised and didn't get their nomination papers in on time and I found myself elected as a councillor without an election.

I suppose it was this sort of 'luck' behind me that caused the local Loughborough party to ask me if I would stand as a candidate in the General Election of 1992 in the very safe Tory seat of Loughborough – it had a majority of over 17,000. It would be good experience, they insisted. It certainly was; I managed to cut the majority to 10,000, increasing the Labour vote by 40 per cent. I was pleased and thought that my brief experience of national politics had been fun. All I had wanted was to be able to tell my grandchildren that I had been a candidate in the 1992 General Election when Neil Kinnock became Prime Minister! It's strange how things turn out.

I married later that year and thought of nothing but settling down, adjusting to our new life together. I was pretty disillusioned; I couldn't believe that the British people had voted for a party that, in my view, didn't believe in society. I wanted to turn my back on politics. I drifted for a time, drawing back to spend time with family, thinking I had reached the pinnacle of my political career.

I got a call from an old friend to see if I would help John Smith in the Labour leadership election that was held after the defeat of the General Election. At this time I was inspired again by the message of social justice so simply explained by John.

Boundary changes followed and the seat I had fought suddenly became the sort of seat we needed to win. I had always said I would only fight in my own area – and the Boundary Commission drew the new borders around the new village we had moved into. My wife and I prayed about it and, once again, without much effort I secured the nomination and the rest, as they say, is history.

So at each stage, God opened doors. I didn't try too hard to open any particular doors myself. Of course, I had to go to the meetings, but I felt that God was with me at every stage – not necessarily that he wanted me to win, but just that I was doing the right thing, and that whatever happened it was meant to be. I have never been a political animal. I can't fix meetings before they happen, or organise 'my people'. I recall somebody saying to me just before the result was given out that I was duly selected that they had never seen a candidate looking so calm. I tried to explain but I don't think he got it at the time. If you know the outcome is already decided what is there to worry about? I had the same sense of calm in the General Elections of 1997 and 2001.

Usually people say to me: surely politics is such a dirty business, how can a Christian be involved? I often point out that the average church council or PCC meeting can be as fractious as any political event, but at least we fall out over the big issues and not over the speed of the organist, and I know who my opponents are before the meeting starts!

Every day I think about how long I should remain an MP, but then I realise that it is not, of course, in my hands. God will decide when my time is up, and whatever lies beyond will be equally challenging and invigorating.

Psalm 16:5-6 is written out in chalk on our kitchen wall. It reminds us both that God has everything in hand. His power is so great that there is never a reason to worry: 'You, Lord, are all I have and you give me all I need, my future is in your hands.'

At each stage I have trusted and put my future in his hands, and now I am able to serve in Westminster. But I do not think for one moment that being an MP is the only way to serve. I am always very conscious that many Christians are able to serve their local communities directly, in much more practical ways than I could ever hope to achieve. But I have also learned that God puts us all in different places to work with each other to create God's kingdom.

I am still no great theologian. I feel I am put to shame by the knowledge of the Bible of so many of my parliamentary colleagues but I do have that simple sense that all of the time God is still opening the doors. He has closed a few too, but I am sure it is for the right reason.

So God has a purpose and he has put me here to serve. I sat in a small living-room when I was 18, wondering what I could do to help the starving in Africa. Over 18 years later I was humbled to be the only MP present at a meeting called to announce the details of the 100 per cent cancellation of debt for the poorest countries. It was a long journey and one that I never expected to make, but God's unchanging provision and wisdom is a wonder to behold.

To produce real moral freedom, God's grace and man's will must co-operate. As God is the prime mover of nature, so also he creates free impulses toward himself and to all good things. Grace renders the will free that it may do everything with God's help, working with grace as with an instrument which belongs to it. So the will arrives at freedom through love, nay, becomes itself love, for love unites with God.

Meister Eckhart

You are behind me
I do not have to turn around.

You are in front of me
I am walking towards you.

You are beside me
more than any abyss and any mountain.

You are in me
I do not have to look elsewhere

With you in me
I can find you everywhere.

J. Scheffler

> *Every revelation of truth felt with interior savour and spiritual joy is a secret whispering of God in the ear of a pure soul.*
>
> *Walter Hilton*

God did not tell us to follow him because he needed our help but because he knew that serving him would make us whole.

Irenaeus

How careful should we be, as we live on God's bounty, to live to his glory.

Matthew Henry

> Have you given yourself yet to the God who wants you and needs you, who has for you a place in his heart of love and in his plan of life, who alone can make you what in your heart of hearts you want to be, who is ready to take you now, just as you are, and with what you have to bring?
>
> D. P. Thomson

God does not care only for totals, aggregates, masses. God cares for you and me, for our loves, our hopes, our aspirations and troubles, as well as for humankind.

Arthur A. Cowan

> God is not in a certain place, but wherever anything is able to come into contact with him there he is present.
>
> Plotinus

Let everyone understand that real love of God does not consist in the tenderness for which usually we long, just because they console us, but in serving God in justice, fortitude of soul and humility.

St. Teresa

I used to ask God to help me. Then I asked if I might help him. I ended up by asking him to do his work through me.

Hudson Taylor

*Let then our first act
every morning be to
make the following resolve for the day:
I shall not fear anyone on earth.
I shall fear only God.
I shall not bear ill-will toward anyone.
I shall not submit to injustice from anyone.
I shall conquer untruth by truth.
And in resisting untruth I shall put up with all suffering.*

>   Mahatma Gandhi

Too many well-intentioned people are so preoccupied with the clatter of effort to do something *for* God that they don't hear him asking that he might do something *through* them.

>   Thomas Kelly

Make a rule, and pray to God to help you keep it, never, if possible, to lie down at night without being able to say, I have made one human being at least a little wiser, a little happier, or a little better this day.

>   Charles Kingsley

Give God thy heart, thy service, and thy gold
The day wears on, and the time is waxing old.

Sundial at Gloucester Cathedral

God has given us two hands, one to receive with and the other to give with. We are not cisterns made for hoarding; we are channels made for sharing.

Billy Graham

God governs the world, and we have only to do our duty wisely, and leave the issue to him.

John Jay

> Pray to God at the beginning of all thy works that thou mayest bring them all to a good ending.
>
> Xenephon

... in the unknown future

Albert Jewell

I used to be very selective when it came to the Psalms because they seemed to be marred by such unchristian sentiments. I could well identify with the Hebrews as they sat down weeping by the rivers of Babylon, unable to sing the Lord's song in a strange land, but when they found their voice it wished the most horrendous fate upon their captors' children! I therefore pitied my Anglican colleagues who were required to read the entire Psalter at Morning and Evening Prayer every month and much preferred the sanitised selection in the *Methodist Hymn Book*.

Two things have happened since to change my view. In the late 1960s I was impressed by a modern paraphrase used in a public service and the preacher kindly made a present to me of the book from which it was taken. *Good Lord, where are you?* by American Lutheran minister Leslie F. Brandt brought home to me the emotional and spiritual honesty of the Psalter. Here is no pietistic cover-up. God is harangued for his absence, indifference, neglect, even cruelty. Raw emotions are plainly expressed whether of joy or sorrow, whether positive or negative.

I came to realise that most psalms in fact boil down to one or more quite basic cries from the human heart: 'Praise the Lord!' 'Thank you!' 'Sorry!' 'Please help – me, or someone else!' With such cries I can readily identify at different times in life. All our changing human moods are to be found reflected in the Psalms without dissembling or pretence. I warm to such honesty.

The other factor in changing my view of the Psalms arose when I spent the final period of my active ministry as Pastoral Director and Senior Chaplain of Methodist Homes for the Aged (now MHA Care Group). In that work I discovered how close to the experience of older people are many of the sentiments expressed in the Psalms. Older Christians identify with that patient waiting for the Lord alluded to in many psalms (eg. Psalm 40:1) and at times they feel driven to demand: 'How long, O Lord, how long?'

The awesome sense of the lifelong providential care of the Lord, celebrated in Psalm 139, resonates in the experience of many older Christians, and many of the verses in this psalm take on a new significance when one's eyes are growing dim. Counting your blessings, in the manner of Psalm 118, is one of the ways in which the depletions and the increasing frailty of old age can be counterbalanced. And few elders are unable to quote Psalm 23 by heart, God's guidance in time past providing the surety for life's final experience and what we trust lies beyond.

An actual historical context can sometimes be established for a particular psalm as in the case of Psalm 137, but this is the exception rather than the rule. Certainly, to seek to place them within the recorded life of King David is largely a fruitless task. However, there is another context that is all-important and that is the context of the corporate worship of the people of God. What the *Methodist Hymn Book* once was for Methodists and the *Book of Common Prayer* was for Anglicans, the Psalter was and remains for the Jewish people: in it they sang of their deliverance in time past and their trust for the future.

We are an ageing population in Britain, and the mainstream churches are ageing at an even faster rate. Life expectancy is extending the whole time; for women it is currently 80 and for men 76. Those in the 65+ age group are set to overtake the under-16s quite soon. The latest statistics from Christian Research in their English church attendance survey for 1998 shows how the age profile of worshipping Methodists has increased to 38 per cent – and we probably all know churches where the figure is 100 per cent. Most other mainstream denominations follow a similar graph. This has led many local churches to concentrate upon keeping and recruiting children and young people – and no one can argue with that. However, all too few give equal consideration to identifying and meeting the spiritual needs of their increasingly elderly congregations.

Whether used for private meditation or in public worship Psalm 71 is manifestly an old person's prayer: indeed, it is given that title in the *Good News Bible*. It is easy to see why for it sets out much of the spiritual agenda of life's later years:

> Even to old age and grey hairs,
> O God, do not forsake me.
>
> (v18)

Aged people feel intensely the need for security, 'a refuge' at a time in life when circumstances can all appear to conspire against them and they recognise they cannot cope on their own (vv1-6). Many say that they will no longer venture out of doors at night. Helpful though the support of other people may be, as we age we are thrown back ultimately upon God alone. In death as in birth we are utterly dependent upon him. It is his 'track record' throughout our life that gives us reassurance for the unknown future. As John Newton's great hymn has it:

> His love in times past forbids us to think
> He'll leave us at last in trouble to sink.

It is usually only in old age that we have the time and leisure to review our lives. I began to write my own autobiography when I was 60 – strictly not for publication and still very incomplete! I think my main intention was to rediscover the meaning, direction and purpose of my life seen as a whole. It has helped me to review my walk with God, my growth and setbacks over the years: to discern the hand of God in it all. It is good, though certainly not easy, to see at least some of the 'fruit' of one's life. The psalmist gives expression to the hope that his life has at least been a good example in v7:

> I have been like a portent to many,
> but you are my strong refuge.

Sadly, however, old age is by no means always a time of unquestioning trust and sure faith. The knowledge that death is that much nearer poses ultimate questions that admit of no easy answers. God can seem distant, uncaring or even totally absent (vv11-12, 18). He can be blamed for the losses and diminishments that ageing brings (v20). Nevertheless the psalmist's feelings fluctuate and wave upon wave of praise interpolate his more negative moods (vv6, 14-16, 22-24).

Older people may sometimes feel dispirited, even guilty, that they are no longer able to do what they once did, and an activist church such as the Methodist Church does not help them in this. However, there are at least two things older people can go on doing, and do better because of their advancing years. The first is to give themselves in worship and lose themselves in the adoration of God who has done all things needful for our salvation:

> My lips will shout for joy
> when I sing praises to you;
> my soul also, which you have rescued.
>
> (v23)

The second is to tell the story of what God has done to future generations (v18). Still being there, in the worshipping community of the people of God, is eloquent testimony in itself. David's harp (v22) is not strictly necessary but a thankful and praising spirit is!

As I move on into my retirement years, I am sure that this psalm will continue to encourage and inspire me.

Thou brightness of eternal glory, thou comforter of the pilgrim soul, with thee is my tongue without voice, and my very silence speaketh unto thee. Come, oh come; for without thee I shall have no joyful day or hour; for thou art my joy, and without thee my table is empty. Praise and glory be unto thee; let my mouth, my soul, and all creatures together, praise and bless thee.

Thomas à Kempis

Thyself, O my God, thyself for thine own sake
   above all things I love.
Thyself as my last end I long for.
Make me therefore in this life present always
   to love thee before all things,
   to seek thee in all things,
and at the last in the life to come
to find and to keep thee for ever.

Thomas Bradwardine

He requires no great matters of us: a little remembrance of him from time to time, a little adoration: sometimes to pray for his grace, sometimes to offer him your sufferings, and sometimes to return him thanks for the favours he has given you, and still gives you, in the midst of your troubles, and to console yourself with him as often as you can.

Brother Lawrence

We should never know the splendour of God's strength unless we knew the utterness of our own weakness. I think you will find that all the discoveries of the soul in regard to the pity and the power and the might and majesty of God have been made by people who have been driven by the desperateness of their own need, and the completeness of their own inadequacy to turn their gaze outward and upward where alone help could be found.

E. H. Hobday

To any of a fearful heart let me say, 'Be strong.' You are living in a universe not made with hands, in a world that is not delivered over to the will of man. You are in God's world. He made it. He keeps it going. He directs it. He knows that you are here, and his eye is upon you. He never slumbers or sleeps. He has not set the sun shining, the stars twinkling, the flowers growing, the birds singing, for nothing. The world will never get beyond his control. You can never wander beyond his care. Behind all is divine purpose, and in it is infinite love. Have confidence in the kindness of God. Build on it and keep yourself in his love.

Fairfields Whitwell

Any form of communication with God is prayer . . . Some [people] communicate with God through music, others through nature or through art in all its forms. Some are helped by other people; some find God in stillness and solitude, others in activity or company. Some are particularly aware of God in their place of work, others feel closer to him at home or in some place of special meaning for them. And 'any form of communication' means whatever we need to say to God too – anger, fear, gratitude, pain, joy, rejection, doubt, fury, loneliness, need, exhaustion – you name it and you can offer it to/shove it at God. If darkness and light are both alike to God, shouting and sleeping are both fine too.

Alison Tomlin

Life is a struggle, but life is beautiful to me. There is joy in knowing that I lie in the hands of God.

Anne Sedgwick

Let us not lose the savour of past mercies and past pleasures; but like the voice of a bird singing in the rain, let grateful memory survive in the hour of darkness.

Robert Louis Stevenson

God of the spirit of kindness,
in the glory of earth and sea and stars,
in the kaleidoscope of colour and shade and shapeliness,
in the patterns of humour and tenderness and touch,
we celebrate your generosity.

Forgive us when we forget the gift in our every breath,
the care that sustains our every moment,
that grace that can transform our every day.

Set us free from the prison of grudging hearts,
mean desires,
resentful spirits,
give us the courage to act with justice and generosity,
and draw us into love that does not calculate
or keep scores.

Kathy Galloway

When, in all our actions, we look upon ourselves as instruments in the hands of God to work out his hallowed designs, we shall act quietly, without anxiety, without hurry, without uneasiness about the future, without troubling about the past, giving ourselves up to the providence of God and relying more on him than on all possible human means. In this way we shall always be at peace, and God will infallibly turn everything to our good, whether temporal or eternal.

Jean-Pierre de Caussade

O God, we thank thee for the world in which thou hast placed us, for the universe whose vastness is revealed in the blue depths of the sky, whose immensities are lit by shining stars beyond the strength of mind to follow. We thank thee for every sacrament of beauty: for the sweetness of flowers, the sound of streams and swelling sea; for far-reaching lands and mighty mountains which rest and satisfy the soul, the purity of dawn which calls to holy dedication, the peace of evening which speaks of everlasting rest. May we not fear to make this world for a little while our home, since it is thy creation, and we ourselves are part of it. Help us humbly to learn its laws and trust its mighty powers.

W. E. Orchard

How should I fear to die?
Have I not seen
The colour of a small butterfly,
The silver sheen
Of breaking waves and of a wood-dove's wings?

Have I not marked the coat
Of mouse and deer,
The shape of flowers, the thrush's speckled throat –
And shall I fear
To fall into the Hand that made these things?

Teresa Hooley

... with us on our journey

Reg Bailey

Dear Vicar,

Last week you said in your sermon how important it was to come to church. I was very hurt by what you said, as I feel you were getting at me. Perhaps you would be good enough to look at my diary below and see how busy I am, and I think you will see I should be excused on these occasions:

Christmas – Sundays before and after; New Year – bit of a head after the party; Easter – to get away for a break; Spring Bank Holiday – weekend away; End of terms (3) – children need a break; Start of terms (3) – we need a break; Anniversary – second honeymoon; Sickness (5) – one per family member; Holiday (3) – self-explanatory; Bad weather – at least a couple of weekends; Unexpected visitors – you can't expect us to walk out, can you; and Football Specials on TV.

That leaves two weekends. So you can count on us to be in church on 28th February and 19th August, unless something unavoidable comes up.

Yours sincerely, etc.

It is a spoof, I know, based on a sketch performed in a church in New York, but it illustrates a point. Some people will make all the excuses in the world as to why they can't get to church. Why do they really not want to come? A brief question-and-answer session with youngsters is probably just as true for adults. 'It's boring.' 'I don't know the songs – they're boring.' 'The talk is dull.' 'The people aren't very friendly.' 'I don't like all the prayers, they're said all funny.'

But it is strange, isn't it? Some people enjoy coming to church. For them it is exciting, uplifting, inspiring, and the people are warm and welcoming. Why do some find it different? Is it the motivation for coming? We come to church to be in the presence of God, to meet with him and others who come also to meet him.

We don't come for the vicar, the music, or the other people. We come to meet with God. If our motivation for coming is right, then it will not be boring or uninspiring. It will be the high point of the week.

Psalm 84 spells out for me the blessing that accrues to the people of God when they are in his presence – wherever the Lord's presence may be encountered. This psalm was my baptism text, and I have found it to be so helpful over the years, as an example of God's promises fulfilled over and over again.

Looking back, of course, I see now that the journey began many years before, but at the time – 1966 – it was as though the journey was just beginning. I was baptised aged 16 at a lively, open Brethren Church in North London. As he stood in chest-high waders, the Elder who baptised me quoted vv11 and 12 from Psalm 84:

> No good thing does the Lord withhold from those who walk uprightly. O Lord of hosts, [blessed] is everyone who trusts in you.

It was the first couple of verses from Scripture that I ever learnt by heart and, in a way, as I look back over my life, I have now a much more rounded view of how God is the source of every blessing. I recognise, too, that most of the psalm lies in front of vv11 and 12, and that my spiritual journey had begun long before my baptism. It had begun at home: not just in the conventional sense of home, but rather in the sense of being with those with whom God's presence dwelt.

If home was the starting point of my spiritual journey, then no wonder I feel that this psalm resonates with me. The longing for home is written all over it. The writer is eager for home, feeling its pull, sensing its sanctuary, and in the first four verses there is a feeling of wistfulness for home. But it is wistfulness not for the building; it is wistfulness for the Lord. The psalmist yearns for God, and will put body, mind and spirit into seeking and experiencing his Lord:

> How lovely is your dwelling-place, O Lord of hosts! My soul longs, indeed it faints for the courts of the Lord . . . [Blessed] are those who live in your house.

The melodic Celtic rendering, 'How lovely is thy dwelling place', based upon this psalm, leaves me with longing for the presence of God, longing like the psalmist to be at home with God. The best homes are places of family relationship and protection, and at the lowest times of my life it has been my Christian family around me that has made me wistful for God's presence again and for God's blessings that flow from his presence. For Christians are beautiful people, despite all of our faults, because to some extent the beauty of the presence of God shines through and radiates to others.

> [Blessed] are those whose strength is in you, in whose heart are the highways to Zion. As they go through the valley of Baca they make it a place of springs; the early rain also covers it with pools. They go from strength to strength; the God of gods will be seen in Zion.

There is something about being in the presence of the Lord that can strengthen us as Christians. Wistfulness is replaced by resolve. Spending time with the Lord every day strengthens us, builds our inner spirit. This time is not all spent in a building, for God is not confined to the temple, he travels with us on our journey and in so doing he blesses us on the way.

Those who dig deep in a dry valley find water to transform desolation into a fertile oasis, showing us that we can find blessings from our hardships. God is the one who sends rain through no one's enterprise, bringing a whole area to life, and, thankfully, he has more than one way of dealing with our dryness.

The third blessing is where I started at my baptism: the content of knowing that God supplies all our needs. God's nature is to give, not withhold, and his gifts are certainly the best that we can receive.

Call me old-fashioned if you like, but I believe that God hears us when we pray. He answers our prayers when our hearts are right with him. He wants us to experience the joy of answered prayer. He has so much for us, more than we can ever realise. He is like a sun and shield to us, giving us comfort on our journey, grace while we travel, glory when we arrive.

But first we have a decision to make. For me it's an easy decision. I'd rather spend one day in the presence of the Lord than a thousand days in his absence. I enjoy being in his company.

There are many choices to make in life. Some are good choices, some are better choices. Life is that way. Most of us don't need help in making choices between good and bad, but we do need help in making choices between good and better or God and best.

Let the psalmist help you decide.

God's existence does not depend on our recollection. Our existence does not depend on his. Thus, when we turn to prayer, it is not so much a question of recollecting God but of preparing to meet him, adjusting our minds and hearts to his greatness. The true recollection begins as we humbly draw near to this wonderful and glorious God, reminding ourselves, as Augustine said, that 'God is wholly in every place, included in no place, not bound with cords (save those of love), not divided into parts, not changeable into several shapes, filling heaven and earth with his present power, and with his never absent nature.'

W. E. Sangster & Leslie Davison

If you keep watch over your heart, and listen for the voice of God and learn of him, in one short hour you can learn more of him than you could learn from man in a thousand years.

John Tauler

A state of mind that sees God in everything is evidence of growth in grace and a thankful heart.

Charles Finney

> *Every morning, lean your arms awhile*
> *Upon the window-sill of heaven,*
> *And gaze upon the Lord.*
>
> *Then, with that vision in your heart,*
> *Turn strong to meet the day.*
>
> Author unknown

Let the Divine mind flow through your mind and you will be happier. I have found the greatest power in the world in the power of prayer. There is no shadow of doubt of that. I speak from my own experience.

Cecil B. de Mille

Thanksgiving is nothing if not a glad and reverent lifting of the heart to God in honour and praise for his goodness.

James R. Miller

The worship most acceptable to God comes from a thankful and cheerful heart.

Plutarch

With hearts responsive
And enfranchised eyes
We thank thee, Lord,
For all things beautiful and good, and true;
For things that seemed not good yet turned to good
For all the sweet compulsions of thy will
That chased, and tried, and wrought us to thy shape;
For things unnumbered that we take of right,
And value first when first they are withheld;
For light and air; sweet sense of sound and smell;
For ears to hear the heavenly harmonies;
For eyes to see the unseen in the seen;
For vision of the Worker in the work;
For hearts to apprehend thee everywhere –
We thank thee, Lord.

John Oxenham

Prayer is not the lone mental activity of one person, but the spiritual relationship between two. And God is more eager from his side, than we from ours. It is communion, keeping in touch. In prayer, the greatest gift of God is himself.

Anonymous

Our Father dwells in tents as well as in temples, but his far abiding place is in the hearts of humankind.

J. Fred Jones

I know not by what methods rare,
But this I know: God answers prayer.
I know not if the blessing sought
Will come in just the guise I thought.
I leave my prayer to him alone
Whose way is wiser than my own.

Eliza M. Hickok

Bless all who worship thee,
From the rising of the sun
Unto the going down of the same.
Of thy goodness, give us;
With thy love, inspire us;
By thy Spirit guide us;
By thy power, protect us;
In thy mercy, receive us,
Now and always.

Fifth century collect

I felt suddenly my heart melting within me, like wax before fire, with love to God my Saviour, and also felt not only love and peace but a longing to be dissolved and be with Christ. There was a cry in my soul, which I was totally unacquainted with before – 'Abba, Father!' I could not help calling God my Father. I knew that I was his child and that he loved me and heard me.

Howell Harris

All that matters is to be at one with the living God
to be a creature in the house of the God of life.

Like a cat asleep on a chair
at peace, in peace
and at one with the master of the house, with the mistress,
at home, at home in the house of the living,
sleeping on the hearth, and yawning before the fire.

Sleeping on the hearth of the living world,
yawning at home before the fire of life
feeling the presence of the living God
like a great reassurance
a deep calm in the heart
a presence
as of a master sitting at the board
in his own and greater being
in the house of life.

D. H. Lawrence

... a God who heals

Tony Trevithick

The problem of pain and suffering has puzzled every generation and most world religions. Individuals have not known whether to blame God for their experiences or to assume that he is punishing the individual or nation because they have disobeyed him. It is therefore understandable that such uncertainty brought an element of fear into the relationship between humanity and God. David's approach to God on this occasion reflects this attitude.

It is quite wrong to criticise David, or whoever wrote the psalm, when so many centuries have passed, when there have been so many copies made and translations completed. Obviously, we do not have the first edition. I do, however, disagree with his use of the words 'anger' and 'wrath' when describing God's attitude. This does not fit in with my understanding of a loving God. I can cope with righteous indignation but anger implies a loss of control.

It is also evident that the Bible, as a whole, reflects on human life with a belief in dualism. There is light and dark, God and Satan, good and bad. It is further assumed that God will reward the good people, and punish the bad people. So, when we turn to the problem of pain and suffering, it is taken for granted that pain is sent by God as a form of punishment.

However, in our modern world, we do not see life in that same way, nor do we see God as a bad-tempered or vindictive God. Therefore, instead of David's approach, I want to picture an understanding, loving and patient God listening to the appeal for help from a faithful disciple who is in pain.

The healing ministry is one of the mysteries of the church, for there is no logic or consistency about the accounts of healing in the Bible, nor since. Pain, anxiety and fear still cause Christian people to doubt God and often to turn on him as if their problems were due to his deliberate imposition of all their ailments. There are also times when the pain seems too difficult to bear, and the thought of death becomes an attractive way of escape. Others have learnt a deeper truth.

Many years ago, when I was being introduced to the ministry of spiritual healing, I was invited to attend a healing surgery in a church in inner-city Birmingham. The first person to enter was an elderly lady, bent over and relying on two walking-sticks to stay upright and obviously coping with considerable pain. When I asked her how long she had been in her present discomfort she answered, 'For many years. I have been coming here each week for at least three years.' I then asked her if, as was obvious, she had not been healed after attending this surgery for so long, why did she still attend? 'Ah,' she said, 'years ago I was dreadful. I could not cope with the pain nor the frustration of increased disability. I made my husband's life a hell and he nearly left me; my daughter and her family did not come and visit me for they could not cope with my aggressive attitude and the tensions that it caused. Then I came here and they have taught me how to look at and understand pain and what has happened to me and, as a result, I have found peace. Now my marriage is all right again and the family are regular in their visits. God has been so good to me!' She did not attend church services and her belief in God was somewhat tenuous but I learnt a great deal from that lady.

Then a few years ago we had a service televised live from our church in Sevenoaks. During the service I interviewed four disabled members of my congregation. The first had had to have a leg amputated; the second had been blind from birth; a third suffered badly from scoliosis and the fourth was a quadriplegic. When I reached the fourth, a man in his early 50s, he said, 'When my wife left me because of the illness and I lost my job as a school-teacher, I used to ask myself the question "Why me?" Then I realised that God was saying to me, "Why not you?" I learnt that, of course, God did not send my illness and since that day I have tried to maintain my Christian faith and example in spite of increasing limitations.'

Finally, let me tell you about Rita, a lovely Christian lady who has had a hard life and who is married to a man with manic depression. She had great problems with her neck and shoulders and had to wear a surgical collar most of the time. She came to our services of wholeness and healing and though there was never any miraculous change there was an improvement and she always thanked me for the atmosphere of peace. Some months later, when she attended her next appointment at the clinic, the doctor asked for X-rays to be taken. When they came back he became annoyed and asked for them to be done again, convinced that some technician had made a mistake. The second batch showed Rita's neck just as clear as the first ones. 'What has happened?' he asked. 'What have you been doing?' Rita told him of the services she had attended. 'I do not understand it,' he said, 'but God has undoubtedly been good to you!'

Psalm 6 can, therefore, still speak to a modern generation, even if some of the words need to be changed. I hope that David would be able to accept this paraphrase:

> Lord, do not be disappointed in me for asking for your help again. I am ill. My whole body is in pain. I need your healing hands laid on me. I am at my wit's end. I have asked for your help several times. How much longer must I wait for your answer? I appeal to your loving kindness – please come quickly and heal me!

I can now understand the temptation of waiting to die in order to be free of pain. But death seems so pointless. No one will thank you for it and I cannot witness to your love from the grave. I am tired out with my own moaning and groaning. Each night I cry myself to sleep. My pillow is wet with tears. I get depressed and doubts creep into my mind. I hear myself saying, 'What have I done to deserve this?'

I know that you have heard my prayers. So please remove these doubts and fears as well as the pain, and remove the worry that they have brought.

Then, those who mock my faith in you will be put to shame and they will realise that you are indeed a God who heals.

Thank you, Lord.

So many people ask questions about God,
so many people ask questions beginning with an 'if'
If God loves us, why suffering?
If God controls, why war?
If God exists, what is the evidence?

So few people turn the questions round
and wonder what God might ask them.
Given love, why do you hate?
Given peace, why do you wreck it?
Given meaning, why do you choose chaos?

Before your greatness, God, I can only be silent.
I keep my mouth tight shut because there is nothing I can say.

Meet me in the depths of my soul and ask your questions of me,
the questions that I cannot answer because I know so little.

Meet me in that numbing despair
*   which finds no meaning nor purpose in life.*
Meet me in my bewilderment
*   when nothing makes sense any more.*
Meet me in the faithlessness
*   which doubts your purpose and your love.*

Ask your questions of me then,
ask them gently but insistently,
like the constant friend
whose arm around my slumped shoulders
reassures me more than words.

Lift me from despair that narrows my vision
until I stand erect and gaze into your future,
in confidence that nothing can separate me from your love,
and ready to take share of the task
you are asking all your people to complete.

                                                            Stephen Orchard

Have you ever taken your fears to God, got the horizons of Eternity about them, looked at them in the light of his love and grace?

> Robert J. McCracken

Never be afraid to doubt, if only you have the disposition to believe.

> *Samuel Taylor Coleridge*

I do not know how the loving Father will bring out the light at last, but he knows, and he will do it.

> *David Livingstone*

How great a God we need, and how much greater is our God than our greatest need.

> Anonymous

Prayer covers the whole of a person's life. There is no thought, feeling, yearning or desire, however long, trifling or vulgar we deem it to be which, if it affects our real interest or happiness, we may not lay before God and be sure of sympathy. His nature is such that our often coming to him does not tire him. The whole burden of the whole life of every person may be rolled on to God and not weary him.

Harriet Ward Beecher

Spiritual power is a hidden power, locked in the silence of the soul. We cannot force it to come at command of will. But when in extremity our strength is as water, our will as the sighing of the wind, when we yield all physical being and lean hard on the spiritual strength within us, the soul's strength rises to assure us as the sun rises over the rim of the night.

Angelo Patri

Everything in life we really accept undergoes a change. So suffering must become Love. This is the mystery. This is what I must do. I must pass from personal love to greater love . . . I must turn to work. I must put my agony into something, change it. 'Sorrow shall be changed into joy.'

Katherine Mansfield

O God, in this thine hour of grace,
   With needy heart and empty hand,
Yet bidden of thee to seek thy face,
   For blessing at thy feet we stand.

Ours are the vows, the frail desires,
   The high resolve to dare and do;
Our flickering faith to thee aspires,
   And passes like the morning dew.

Ours is the mighty need of thee –
   How great, thy love alone can know;
Ours but the hunger and the plea
   That strives and will not let thee go.

Thy word we clasp, thy touch we wait;
   Our eyes, O God, are unto thee,
Whose loving-kindness makes us great
   Whose strength shall seal our victory.

C. H. Boutflower

Trust God when you cannot trace him. Do not try to penetrate the cloud; rather look to the bow that is on it. The mystery is God's; the promise is yours.

John Macduff

You cannot live on what God did yesterday; therefore he comes today.

John Wesley

O Lord, I cannot see!
Vouchsafe me light:
The mist bewilders me,
Impedes my sight:
Hold thou my hand, and lead me by thy side:
I dare not go alone: be thou my guide.

        Jane Saxby

God doesn't always smooth the path, but sometimes he puts springs in the wagon.

        Anonymous

> *What is soiled, make thou pure;*
> *What is wounded work its cure;*
> *What is parched fructify*
> *What is rigid, gently bend;*
> *What is frozen, warmingly tend;*
> *Strengthen what goes erringly.*
>
>   *Anonymous, 13th century*

O heart, lay down thy troubles! Look up to God! Who trusts in him is safe.

       A German pastor in prison

... there in the mess and turmoil of life

Eluned Williams

As a child and a young person, growing up and nurtured in the Welsh-speaking Presbyterian Church of Wales, one of the outstanding memories I have of weekly morning worship was the Chant. Every Sunday we sang a psalm which even then, to a child, seemed to enrich the worship. In more recent years, through ecumenical opportunities, I occasionally find myself in situations, particularly in Anglican settings, when these childhood memories become real once again when a psalm is sung.

The majority of the Psalms lend themselves to being chanted without great difficulty and I rejoice when this opportunity is presented. I would happily welcome a return of this practice as part of our weekly worship!

I hail from a culture where we learned the Psalms in Sunday school so that we could both recite and chant them from memory. This was a part of our Eisteddfodic tradition. The Book of Psalms was a popular resource for both individual and choral speaking or chanting competitions. Consequently, passages frequently return to my memory.

I am so very fortunate to live in an area of outstanding beauty: at the foot of a majestic mountain range yet only nine miles inland from the coast and the rolling breakers of the sea. So many aspects of passages from the Psalms can so easily be related to the changing moods of this physical environment. Likewise it is easy to relate this to one's personal mood, according to circumstances and pressures. I sometimes find myself walking in open countryside, making my way up a mountainside or battling against a strong westerly wind whilst struggling to walk along a deserted beach in winter, and passages from the Psalms come, uninvited, into my mind. It is good to say, or sing, the words out loud; one can do this uninhibited in deserted places.

Many of the Psalms relate to the wonder and awesomeness of God's creation, while others give expression to the struggles and challenges which we often find ourselves facing as we journey through life. Some Psalms reflect feelings of desertion, whilst others speak of cities, associated with uproar and rush, change and challenge.

One of my favourite psalms is Psalm 46. 'God is our refuge and strength, a very present help in trouble' are the opening words, whilst the closing words reflect the whole reassurance of the psalm: 'The Lord of hosts is with us; the God of Jacob is our refuge.' The stanzas in between reflect turbulence and trauma, challenge and chaos, but then we read, 'Be still, and know that I am God! I am exalted among the nations, I am exalted in the earth.' These words reflect not only something of the turbulence of nature, but also something of the upheaval of people's lives.

In my work with children and young people over a long period of time, I realised, as I reflected on the turbulence and trauma of their lives, that the only source of any real healing, leading to wholeness, is indeed scriptural and God-given.

The pain and hurt of humans is always something of a devastating experience for those who work at depth with them, and this is even more so when applied to children, whose innocence and dependence, trust and sense of discovery can be shattered before they reach maturity.

As I discovered, and as is to be anticipated, the greater the damage, the more difficult and complex the healing. Indeed, sometimes the carer needed to probe the hurt so deeply to enable that healing to occur, in order to lead to a 'letting go' of the hurt, to move on and to grow.

'Be still, and know that I am God.' This is such a reassuring message. But how can one be still when there is so much internalised anger and hurt?

This psalm reflects something of that message for me, ending as it does with such reassurance. Extreme anger can be a destructive force, especially in a young person, whose greatest desire is to be loved. The parameters offered by the words of this psalm suggest a blueprint for the expression of controlled anger within a safe environment and the constant message of reassurance woven throughout. In such work with damaged children and young people, symbolism is a tool one seeks to use skilfully. Psalm 46 offers a very lovely, yet strong, symbol of healing and wholeness.

The same symbol is also reflected in nature. 'There is a river where streams make glad the city of God.' We are well-used to the healing symbolism of flowing water. In Welsh, the words 'Y mae afon a'i ffrydiau 'n llawenhau dinas Duw' are frequently sung, and the musical setting has in itself a healing tone. 'There is a river whose streams make glad the city of God.' This is a powerful image on to which I have held whilst undertaking healing work with disturbed children. When the stream becomes a raging torrent, after heavy rain, it is a powerful, destructive force. It rushes down the mountainside, even leaving its normal course, becoming discoloured as it churns up the earth, taking with it anything in its path. It is no longer recognised as the gentle stream which offers water for thirsty cattle and sheep, which feeds the lush greenery alongside its path, which gently washes over stones and rocks, highlighting the rich colours of the minerals within the rock strata, which soothes tired and aching feet after a day's hiking. The water described by the psalmist is a healing symbol – a river with tributary streams able to gently wash, clean and purify.

Part of the healing process for those who are hurting is for them to be able to pass on their pain; to free themselves of it; to allow others to carry the cross which weighs them down and causes them to stumble, which disables them as they struggle to be still, to find an inner stillness and peace. God is indeed our refuge and strength – both for the victim and the healer. So when lives suffer tumultuous shaking as described in the psalm, the reassurance of the safety and refuge God offers is overwhelming.

Many of us come face to face with difficult situations which are painful, but one of the most devastating and damaging aspects of human relationships must be rejection, especially when a child's feeling of rejection is reinforced by negative vibes and damaging behaviour and circumstances. So when placed in a safe environment the child tests that situation to ensure that rejection will not be repeated. In fact it is an obtuse way of inviting rejection – a classic symptom.

For me, Psalm 46 rings with the reassurance that there is no need for us to test God as he remains constant in his relationships, in his promises. During the times when I was close to contemplating giving up with a particular child, I drew strength from the words of this psalm. In my heart I knew such an action would be yet another rejection, adding to the existing destruction. The overwhelming message contained in Psalm 46 is that God is there in the midst of the mess and turmoil which is a part of life. His constant love offers security whatever befalls us. His healing power is as the river whose streams make glad the city of God and brings music into our souls.

> God is our refuge and strength . . .
> The Lord of hosts is with us;
> > the God of Jacob is our refuge.

During my professional career, this psalm became for me an additional valuable tool, without which the expertise which I hoped to bring to my healing ministry would have been far less powerful and meaningful.

When we say, 'God is our refuge and strength, a very present help in trouble', we recognise that we need the refuge, the strength, and the help which God alone can give. Instead of attempting to escape from life, we turn and look it full in the face, and we have to admit that there are forces around us and within us which are stronger than we are; forces with which we ourselves are quite inadequate to deal.

Raymond Abba

In all created things discern the providence and wisdom of God, and in all things give him thanks.

Teresa of Avila

God's majesty speaks to us by the works of his almighty hands.

R. H. Benson

The fruit that silence brings is known to the person who has experienced it. God has led us into solitude to speak to our heart.

Bruno of Cologne

How can you expect God to speak in that gentle and inward voice which melts the soul, when you are making so much noise with your rapid reflections? Be silent, and God will speak again.

Francois Fenelon

Let me be mindful of God's splendour,
not only in those quiet half hours
plucked from the day between sleeping and rising,
from the silent room on peaceful evenings,
with books outspread.
But as I rush through the world,
race through that strident turbulence
of urgency and incidence,
let me so carry God's great glory
like a torch in my hand,
a sun in my face,
a flame in my heart,
that people may turn in their tracks,
feeling the warmth of it,
catching the light.

Oh, let my pillar of fire be seen
burning clearly in the confusion,
and not only in those quiet half hours
with books outspread.

Virginia Thesiger

To 'be still' is something which many of us are not very good at in these early days of the 21st century. There is pressure on us, always, to be looking ahead rather than living in and savouring the moment we have. Our lives are ruled by the clock: we must get to work, go home again to care for family members, to complete chores, to prepare for tomorrow. Even our days off are crammed with activity, and our church lives often become as full as we scurry from service, to committee meeting, to prayer group.

But God's command is that we should 'be still'. To be really still is immensely therapeutic. It encourages us to relax and be calm, allowing our heartbeat to slow, our tensed muscles and emotions to be at rest. It helps us to feel that, for a short time, we are stepping back to rest and to allow ourselves to be restored.

Anonymous

Humility is the perfect quietness of heart . . . It is to have a blessed home in the Lord, where I can go in and shut the door and kneel to my Father in secret, and am at peace as in the deep sea of calmness when all around and above is trouble.

Andrew Murray

I place myself and all my affairs lovingly in the hands of my Father. That which is for my highest good shall come to me.

Evelyn Whitell

Let us, then, labour for an inward silence –
An inward stillness and an inward healing;
That perfect silence where the lips and heart
Are still, and we no longer entertain
Our own imperfect thoughts and vain opinions,
But God alone speaks in us, and we wait
In singleness of heart, that we may know
His will and in the silence of our spirits,
That we may do his will, and do that only.

                Henry Wadsworth Longfellow

Have you stood alone on some hilltop at midnight, when the great lamp of heaven is shining down on the silent earth, and the valley stretches out for miles and miles beneath your feet, and not a leaf stirring, not a soul is moving, not a bird is singing? You were alone with the stars. Is anything so dramatic as that? We marvel at the power of the kingdoms of humankind, but we stand in awe at the solemn stillness of the kingdom of God. To stand alone in some great place, in some great hour with all the world shut out save for the everlasting wonder of the stars, is to feel that silence on the earth in which there seems to come to us as the voice of angels. We hear the music of the spheres; we hear a voice that seems to say, 'Be still, and know that I am God . . .'

                        The Children's Newspaper

O God, who art the author of love, and the lover of pure peace and affection, let all who are terrified by fears, afflicted by poverty, harassed by tribulation, worn down by illness, be set free by thy tenderness, raised up by amendment of life, and cherished by thy daily compassion.

Gallican Sacramentary

> When you have shut the doors and made a darkness within; remember never to say that you are alone; for you are not alone, but God is within.
>
> Epicetus

Faith, like light, should always be simple and unbending, while love, like warmth, should beam forth on every side, and bend to every necessity of our brothers and sisters.

Martin Luther

... the strength of my heart

Harold Good

There will be few of us who at some time in our lives have not felt aggrieved or frustrated at what we have seen to be the blatant unfairness of life. How is it that those who try to live a decent life often appear to suffer more than those who have little or no respect for God or for his rules for living?

The family of the young mother, yet another victim of cruel cancer, will have good reason to wonder why she should be 'taken' from her children while convicted rogues and rascals roam the streets.

An honest trader, whose business goes to the wall when he refuses to compromise, cannot but wonder when he sees an unscrupulous competitor survive and prosper.

The conscientious student who has 'spurned delights and lived laborious days' to achieve a result of which both she and her parents will be justly proud, will find it difficult to see the coveted award go to one who has given scarce time to study and whose thesis has been largely 'borrowed' from an unacknowledged source.

Why submit oneself to the rigorous discipline of a healthy lifestyle when so many who are careless and self-indulgent will outlive their 'good living' and health-conscious neighbours?

Imagine the feelings of the police widow, struggling with her grief and the enormous demands of single motherhood, when she sees the perpetrators of terror walk freely through her small town.

This was exactly the dilemma of the author of Psalm 73.

> For I was envious of the arrogant; I saw the prosperity of the wicked.
>
> (v3)

> Such are the wicked, always at ease, they increase in riches. All in vain I have kept my heart clean . . . For all day long I have been plagued . . .
>
> (vv12-14)

We share the puzzlement of the saintly soul, faithful in worship and service to her local church and community, now imprisoned in her home, trapped in a disabled body, suffering intolerable pain, who from her window observes the activities of those who live only unto themselves.

> For they have no pain; their bodies are sound and sleek . . . they are not plagued like other people.
>
> (vv4-5)

This is what makes the Book of Psalms so real. In poetic language, the psalmist shares the honest feelings we may be reluctant to express and asks those painful questions for which there are no easy answers.

What does the pastor say to good folk who constantly wonder about what they see to be the unfairness of life and the justice of God? What can we learn from the psalmist who, when it all gets too much for him, goes to the quiet place in his search for an answer? To begin with, things are not always as they appear to be.

> But when I thought how to understand this, it seemed to me a wearisome task, until I went into the sanctuary of God; then I perceived their end.
>
> (v17)

In this quiet time of reflection, the psalmist begins to realise that those whom we are tempted to envy are not quite as secure as he (or we) first thought they were!

> Truly you set them in slippery places; you make them fall into ruin. How they are destroyed in a moment, swept away utterly by terrors! They are like a dream when one awakes; on awaking you despise their phantoms.
>
> (vv18-20)

Some things don't change. In our time, from our newspapers and our small screens, we are very familiar with sad stories of men and women whose fantasies about their own self-sufficiency have been fleeting and whose apparent prosperity has floundered upon 'slippery slopes' of one kind or another.

But, as Christians, do we take delight in the misfortune of others? Can we take satisfaction in the knowledge that anyone should be destroyed and swept away by terrors?

Not so, if we are to interpret correctly the mind and spirit of Jesus who made it so clear that he had not come to call the righteous, but sinners to repentance; he who prayed for those who scoffed at him in his suffering from their position of apparent security, short-lived though it turned out to be.

In this, there is no fundamental contradiction between the psalmist and what is required of us by Christ. The psalmist is simply echoing the confusion of the person who struggles with his or her human feelings at a time when his heart was grieved and his spirit embittered (v21).

To deny such feelings is to deny our humanity, something that Jesus never did. But, moving beyond his understandable feelings of resentment, the psalmist realises that the fate of the proud, the arrogant and the wicked is a matter for God, and not for him. What matters to him, and therefore to us, is the experience of the secure and loving providence of God.

> . . . you hold my right hand. You guide me with your counsel, and afterwards you will receive me with honour. Whom have I in heaven but you? And there is nothing on earth that I desire other than you. My flesh and my heart may fail, but God is the strength of my heart and my portion forever.
>
> (v23-26)

On 8th November 1987, Remembrance Sunday, in the town of Enniskillen, Co. Fermanagh, 11 people lost their lives in a brutal bombing of the annual service at the cenotaph. The story of Gordon Wilson holding the hand of his dying daughter, Marie, as they lay buried under the rubble, touched the world, particularly his plea for healing and his offer of forgiveness to those who had taken the life of his child. Supported by the love and the prayers of his wife, Joan, Gordon gave himself unstintingly to the cause of peace and reconciliation in Northern Ireland. Within a short time, their beloved son, Peter, died in a tragic accident, leaving his young wife, Ingrid, with their two small daughters. Not long afterwards, undaunted but exhausted, Gordon suffered a massive coronary from which he died at the height of his crusade for peace.

On a recent Sunday evening, as Methodist President, I visited the Enniskillen Circuit. Mid-way through the service there was a solo by Ingrid, accompanied by Gordon's widow, Joan. Contrary to what would have been understandable, their song was not of pain and grief and confusion, but of the love and the grace of a providential God in whom, like the psalmist, they had found 'their refuge'. They wanted only to sing and 'tell of all [his] works' (v28).

Much as we might wish it to be otherwise, no amount of personal faith will provide a guarantee of protection against the potential suffering and pain of this life. If this were so, the whole world would come to faith overnight!

Would we really want a relationship that is conditional upon the promise of reward in terms of good health and/or fortune? In a loving marriage we give ourselves to one another for better or for worse, in sickness and in health. This is what makes any relationship special.

The timeless biblical promise is that there is simply nothing, in life or in death, which can separate us from the love of God made real to us in Jesus Christ our Lord.

It does look as though the wicked [are] having a good time. There are no pangs in their death; they have an easy time. The righteous are again and again seen battered and bruised with life, until . . . until when? Until they go to the sanctuary of God, the true viewpoint for life. When we get to the sanctuary of God life is seen in its long issues and never measured by immediate appearances.

George Campbell Morgan

Throughout the Bible God appears as the liberator of the oppressed. He is not neutral. He does not attempt to reconcile the Hebrew slaves with their Egyptian oppressors or to reconcile the Jewish people with any of their later oppressors. Oppression is sin and it cannot be compromised with, it must be done away with. God takes sides with the oppressed. As we read in Psalm 103:6, 'God, who does what is right, is always on the side of the oppressed.'

Kairos Document

God is not one thing because he is, and another thing because he is just; with him to be just and to be God are one and the same.

Boethius

The love that kept us through the passing night will guide and keep us still.

Anonymous

If a man is centred upon himself, the smallest risk is too great for him, because both success and failure can destroy him. If he is centred upon God, then no risk is too great, because success is already guaranteed – the successful union of Creator and creature, beside which everything else is meaningless.

                                                Morris West

What, then, shall we do when our illusions leave us? The Scriptures have much to say for the consolation of the disillusioned. They urge people to lift up their eyes from the broken toys that have disappointed them, to the splendours that endure for evermore.

                                                F. W. Boreham

O God, who tellest the number of stars, and callest them all by their names; heal, we beseech thee, the contrite in heart, and gather together the outcasts, and enrich us with the fullness of thy wisdom, through Christ our Lord.

                                                Sarum Breviary

Pain is the deepest thing we have in our nature, and union through pain and suffering has always seemed more real and holy than any other.

Arthur Hallam

O God our Father, hear me, who am trembling in this darkness, and stretch forth thy hand; hold forth thy light before me; recall me from my wanderings; and, thou being my guide, may I be restored to myself and thee.

St. Augustine

Sometimes great difficulties are permitted only in order to strengthen character.

R. H. Benson

Sorrow and suffering demand a quieter expression of faith. We face an uncertain future knowing that *all* our life is God's concern and God's care. Our times are in his hands. That is enough. We put our trust in him.

Leslie Church

Calamity can never completely overwhelm us. His presence can make our darkness light, and though we may be stricken to the ground, he will wait until it is time to raise us up.

Source unknown

> I have never committed the least matter to God, that I have not had reason for infinite praise.
>
> Anna Shipton

The wind passes, and it bends – let the wind, too, pass over the spirit. From the cloud-shadow it emerges to the sunshine – let the heart come out from the shadow of the roofs to the open glow of the sky. High above, the songs of the larks fall as rain – receive it with open hands. Pure is the colour of the green flags – let the thought be pure as the light that shines through that colour. Broad are the downs and open the aspect – gather the breadth and largeness of the view. . . One memory of the green corn, fresh beneath the sun and wind will lift up the heart from the clouds.

Richard Jeffries

> *Prayer is a rising up and a drawing near to God in mind, and in heart, and in spirit.*
>
> Alexander Whyte

O Lord our God, the stay of all them that put their trust in you, wherever you lead we would go, for your ways are perfect wisdom and love. Be our Friend, and we need ask no more in heaven or earth, in youth or age, for you are the comfort of all who put their trust in you. O Lord, we would be yours, keep us in your love and truth, guide us by your Holy Spirit.

S. Weiss (adapted)

I believe in God, and in his wisdom and benevolence.

Anonymous

Gracious God, transform our dullness with the colours of your love and help us to bring brightness to the dark places of the world through hope.

Source unknown

... the source of life

David Beazley

O Lord, you have searched me and you know me. There is such comfort in that, such eternal hope. You perceive my thoughts from afar . . . you are familiar with all my ways. In my Lord I have one who understands me from beneath the depths of my lowest states to the height of my joyous fulfilments; from the confident strengths of my certainties to the empty awfulness of my doubts. In sin and sorrow and shame I have one into whose arms I can run, rather than needing to run away; one who sees me even though I might seek refuge from him – who is himself the only true and safe refuge. He knows me fully, and yet he loves me. What utter safety there is in that; I know of no other such hiding-place. What point would there be in running, escaping, hiding? Where could I go to escape from his presence, even if I longed to? Though I may go down to the depths, deliberately or unwittingly, even there his right hand will hold me fast.

In the depths of despair and disease, of brokenness and doubt, of rebellion and anger; and in the heights of comfort and confidence, of joy and fulfilment, of forgetfulness and presumption, his hand will guide me if I but remember his fundamental authorship of my life and turn to him again. No, I may not be suddenly released from my pain, nor robbed of my prosperity. But to acknowledge him, and know the timeless dimension of his acknowledgement of me, his child, is to get back onto an eternal course that transcends the human condition.

I have had the privilege of some involvement with the Leprosy Mission, and have felt that the disease illustrates well the human condition that Psalm 139 describes. Leprosy is an awful thing – at least it was thought to be, and if feared and concealed, untreated and stigmatised, it still can be. But now, by God's grace and the wonder of medicine, it is curable, and its devastating effects preventable, if it is found and treated in time. It is interesting how the Bible portrays leprosy (and there were other conditions the ancients put under the same name) as an affliction fearful enough to warrant shame and banishment, religious uncleanness and imputations of sin. Scripture has left us – albeit unintentionally – with an image of a disease which has a spiritual parallel, an allegory of our spiritual condition, as if our sin were like a leprosy of the soul, a deadly danger if undiagnosed, concealed and untreated.

The symptoms are the same: a mysteriously contracted, slow-developing disease, a condition which dulls sensation, so that I damage myself without realising, and cause infection, disability and deformity to begin to creep in. Only then do I see what is happening, and if I know not what to do or where to go, or dare not or cannot admit my need, then to hide or flee and be turned away is my only option.

Leprosy and sin have parallels, (although, of course, we would no longer suggest they are linked). 'If I say, "Surely the darkness will hide me and the light become night around me . . ." ' The stigma and ignorance surrounding leprosy have caused countless sufferers to seek the darkness at the edges of society, the far side of the sea in their isolation and loneliness. Thousands have made their bed in the depths, concluding that they are rejected, cursed, unwanted; lives wasted, hopelessness bone-deep in body, mind and spirit. And so it can also be with our spiritual condition, our felt need and all-too human response to it.

Yet the psalmist says that God created my inmost being; I am fearfully and wonderfully made. I was not hidden from him, even before birth. In the depths of the earth, in the secret place, God knit me together in my mother's womb. Surely I was made for more than the life-wasting ravages of disease, physical, mental, emotional or spiritual.

There is a cure. If I seek it early, I can live again with no scar, no disability, no anaesthetic limbs, no deformities, no blindness. And even if I have left it too late to avoid those effects, although I may have fled away for too long, on the wings of my dawn, on the far side of my sea, in the depths of my bed: even there God can reach me and hold me fast, his hand can guide me out. He can heal, he can cleanse, he can restore and I can live again, with dignity, with value, with acceptance, with purpose, with love.

God's thoughts for me are those of my maker, the parent of my whole being, the author who was active long before the biological process which put his loving plan into action. His eyes saw my unformed body. What a precious thought; such knowledge is too wonderful for me. God not only can but does love me, and lays his hand upon me from long before my birth through into eternity. He hems me in, he is all around me, above, beneath, before, beyond. How vast is the sum of all his thoughts – about me, even me. And when you add every last precious created child in the teeming mass of humanity, those thoughts of my Lord's outnumber the grains of sand. The rich Westerner with spiritual senses threatened by wealth and comfort, the beautiful young thing deluded by ease and happiness, or the victim of oppression and injustice, the sufferer of pain and disability, the countless children of God – all of us afflicted by a leprosy of the soul – his heart is for us all. And he has given a cure, for the darkness is not darkness to him, and through his Son he has flooded us with a light into which we can come by his grace alone.

The sudden change in the mood of the psalmist in verses 19-22 speaks of an enemy. Perhaps the writer had a human, physical threat in mind, but Jesus tells us rather to fear those who can kill the soul as well. So here is the real enemy, who stigmatises you, who writes you off in rejection, isolation, hopelessness, just as people wrote off the leprosy sufferers of old. This enemy hates the Lord who loves you, whatever affliction has done to you, wherever you have gone to hide, whatever lies you have absorbed about your worthlessness and sin beyond redemption.

'Search me, O God, and know my heart, test me and know my anxious thoughts. See if there is any offensive way in me, and lead me in the way everlasting.' Offensive way? There is only one fundamental offensive way: it is the way which wants to lead me away from God, which causes me to try to flee, to hide, to run from the reality of my need for healing, for acceptance, for love, for dignity, for fulfilment, for God.

O God, there is such peace in knowing that all my days are already known – written in your book, and that I don't have the worry of knowing their number! A life begun as I was woven together in the secret place under your loving gaze, a life touching this human world just for those days whose number you already know. Let me not use this brief time to fall victim to any of the world's countless leprosies, nor flee from your Spirit in my shame and anger and confusion, nor in my wealth and comfort. And then, one day, I will turn to sleep, and when I wake I will still be with you. I love you, Lord, because you love me so comprehensively; you gave my life value because it is your life, you made it, dignified it, gave it potential. And then you died to win it back from loss.

Lord, you have searched me and you know me. There is such comfort in that; such eternal hope.

I come to thee, great King, a humble suppliant,
And bow me low beneath thy mercy seat,
And ask thee for the gift of perfect silence,
For me, of all people, this prayer most meet.

So would I worship thee in utter reverence,
Nor say one word nor lift my eyes to thee,
But wrap me in the mantle of my silence
And lay quite still before thy majesty.

Silence of reverence and true obedience,
Thy creature's will responding to thy will,
Love sitting at the feet of her Creator,
Because she knows thee, learning to be still. Amen.

Anonymous

What do we mean by grace? The old definition called it 'the free, unmerited favour of God'. On that definition I cannot improve. It means that at the heart of all true communion with God there lies this deep truth – that God himself took the initiative. He loves us better than we can ever love him. He loves us with a love that does not depend on any answering love of ours. We have not to earn his love . . . we have but to receive it.

W. E. Sangster

Be not afraid of life. Believe that life is worth living, and your belief will help create the fact.

William James

Every time you pray, if your prayer is sincere, there will be new feeling and new meaning in it which will give you fresh courage.

Feodor Dostoevsky

In all that happens God is present, though not all that happens carries his presence in its fullness. In the event that we consider evil, all that we may be able to see of his presence is his permission that life in this place should just now have this dreadful character. He is also present in the redeemability that lies deep within every evil. It is part of the goodness of life that every evil carries this whisper of God. He is indeed everywhere. There is a psalm that says that even if you made your bed in hell you would lie down with God.

J. Neville Ward

Yesterday now is part of forever,
Bound up in a sheaf which God holds tight,
With glad days and sad days and bad days, which never
Shall visit us more with their bloom and their blight,
Their fullness of sunshine or sorrowful night.
Let them go, since we cannot retrieve them,
Cannot undo and cannot atone;
God in his mercy forgive; receive them!
Only the new days are our own –
Today is ours and today alone.

Source unknown

There is a sense in which we must forgive ourselves our own sins, by which I mean, we must put them behind our backs. If God has put them behind his, we are not to go poking about behind his back dragging out our sins and wearing them round our neck again . . . When you have faced your own sin, put right anything that you can put right, realise that the relationship is restored, that you are starting again, a new person, that whatever you suffer is remedial discipline, not retributive punishment, put it behind your back, then it can be forgotten, you have 'cleansed and called home your spirit'.

Leslie Weatherhead

The peace of God . . . is a peace that banishes all doubt, all painful uncertainty, the Spirit bearing witness with the spirit of a Christian, that he [or she] is a child of God.

John Wesley

It fortifies my soul to know
That though I perish, truth is so;
That whereso'er I stray and range
Whate'er I do, thou dost not change.
I steadier step when I recall
That, if I slip, thou dost not fall.

Arthur Hugh Clough

. . . If it makes sense to speak of God at all, then we must be able to experience God in the centre of our lives where we spend most of our time and expend most of our energy. To realise that God is there in the centre of our lives at the deepest dimension of every human moment means that God is never far from us. To experience God in the depths is to be aware that we are related to a larger mystery within which we live.

Richard M. Gula

> *I had a thousand questions to ask God, but when I met with him they all fled and didn't seem to matter.*
>
> *Christopher Morley*

Psalm 139 is a prayer of praise and thanksgiving which humbly acquiesces to God's personal knowledge of each of us. It helps us to understand more clearly how intimately God is present to us.

The psalmist proclaims that God created him with infinite care and formed him in the divine likeness. Here and in Hebrews 4:13 the writer acknowledges God's wisdom which knows the attitudes and thoughts of the heart. God is so intimately present to us that nothing can be hidden.

For some this thought could be frightening, for it might project an ever-watchful God who scrutinises and records all that we say and do. On the other hand the certainty of God's presence can be joyful, for it underlines the care God has for us. Recognising this God who is inside us nurturing us and outside us challenging us as we are enveloped by love can lead us to greatness as we live life fully and intensely. . .

Sometimes it is hard to see ourselves as God sees us, to love ourselves as God loves us. We have somehow learned to be afraid of God rather than to feel secure in God's presence. To love ourselves as God loves us means learning to trust that the God who created us is the One who will never let us go.

Loretta Girzaitis

God is great, and therefore he will be sought: he is good and therefore he will be found.

Anonymous

... worthy of praise

Briant Smith

Lord, your presence fills this place;
the heavy cloud and lack of wind
give an intensity of atmosphere
which is hard to take in.
No human sound invades the mystery;
the sense of you in this place.
Here from the beginning of time,
and still present today.
From this point high above the sea and surrounding land,
a few houses are visible,
but the impact of human hand is minimal.
The vastness of the sea, the majesty of the scenery,
and the changing patterns of cloud and sky,
all testify to your greatness,
your creative power, Lord,
and they make me pause and wonder.
And yet, here in my loneliness and isolation
I also feel your very closeness,
drawing me to you in the silence.
Lord, may I always be aware
of your still, small voice saying to me
'Here I am, come to me:
in the vastness of creation I have a special place for you,
and you are precious to me.'
I can only respond by reopening my heart
and my spirit to you in thankful praise.

The piece is part of an ongoing quest to develop a spirituality of the countryside; a search for the Creator through the wonders of his creation. As well as being a significant part of my own personal journey the desire is to encourage others to stop and stare, and to allow God to speak to us through the beauty and the quiet. This particular prayer was written while looking at Bardsey Island, (Ynys Enlli in Welsh), also known as the Island of 20,000 saints, which is situated at the tip of the Lleyn peninsular in North-West Wales, and was the destination for many pilgrims in the past, and maintains its special, and peaceful, spirituality to this day.

> *The mystery of God has exercised [a] strange fascination over the human mind almost from the dawn of time. And great religious thinkers have ransacked human language for images which convey this strange, elusive sense of the Wholly Other who emerges from dazzling darkness to haunt our lives. Plato talked of flickering shadows on the wall of a cave; Isaiah, in a beautiful image, described God as passing by and there was nothing to be seen, but those who listened carefully could hear the rustle of his garments as he swept past – the whisper of God's ways.*
>
> *Colin Morris*

As we were going along, we were stopped at the distance of perhaps 50 yards from our favourite birch tree. It was yielding to the gusty wind . . . The sun shone upon it. It was a tree in shape, with stem and branches, but it was like a spirit!

Dorothy Wordsworth

Joy is the holy fire that keeps our purpose warm and our intelligence aglow.

Helen Keller

We thank thee, Lord, for this fair earth,
The glittering sky, the silver sea;
For all their beauty, all their worth,
Their light and glory, come from thee.

Thanks for the flowers that clothe the ground,
The trees that wave their arms above,
The hills that gird our dwellings round,
As thou dost gird thine own with love.

Yet teach us still how far more fair,
More glorious, Father, in thy sight,
Is one pure deed, one holy prayer,
One heart that owns thy Spirit's might.

So, while we gaze with thoughtful eye
On all the gifts thy love has given,
Help us in thee to live and die,
By thee to rise from earth to heaven.

George Cotton

What God has resolved concerning me I know not, but this I least I know: he has instilled into me a vehement love of the beautiful.

John Milton

Suddenly the Thing happened, and, as everybody knows, it cannot be described in words. The Bible phrase, 'I saw the heavens open' seems as good as any if not taken literally. I remember saying to myself, in awe and rapture, 'So it's like this; now I know what heaven is like, now I know what they mean in church.' The words of the 23rd Psalm came into my head and I began repeating them: 'he maketh me to lie down in green pastures; he leadeth me beside the still waters.' Soon it faded and I was alone in the meadow with the baby and the brook and the sweet-smelling lime trees. But though it passed and only the earthly beauty remained, I was filled with great gladness. I had seen the 'far distances'.

Margaret Isherwood

Gratitude to God makes even a temporal blessing a taste of heaven.

William Romaine

For worship is a thirsty land crying for rain;
It is a candle in the act of being kindled.
It is a voice in the night calling for help.
It is a soul standing in awe before the mystery of the universe,
It is a time flowing into eternity . . .
. . . a person climbing the altar stairs to God.

Author unknown

The whole world is a phylactery, and everything we see is an item of the wisdom, power, or goodness of God.

> Thomas Browne

> God of the granite and the rose,
> Soul of the sparrow and the bee,
> The mighty tide of being flows
> Through countless channels, Lord, from thee.
>
> > Elizabeth Doten

'How do you know,' a Bedouin asked, 'that there is a God?' 'In the same way,' was the reply, 'that I know, on looking at the sand, when a person or a beast has crossed the desert – by his footprints in the world around me.'

> Henry Parry Liddon

God is, and all is well.

> *John Greenleaf Whittier*

The skies were mine, and so were the sun and moon and stars, and all the world was mine; and I the only spectator and enjoyer of it.

Thomas Traherne

We can learn to see the beautiful, and to reproduce it, in our thoughts, feelings and acts.

Frank Crane

When a person turns their open life to God so that he may make himself known, God becomes real to the soul. In the nature of things, 'meeting' and 'finding' at the personal level can happen only in that way. Just as friendship can be proved only by entering into it, so God's existence can be proved only by entering into relationship with him. When we move into the realm of personality we meet with a kind of reality which cannot be registered or tested by purely rational means, but only by tasting it, experiencing it. It is to this order of reality that our awareness of God's existence belongs.

Eric G. Frost

I walked abroad alone, in a solitary place in my father's pasture, for contemplation. And as I was walking there, and looked upon the sky and clouds, there came into my mind a sweet sense of the glorious majesty and grace of God that I knew not how to express.

Jonathan Edwards

CONTRIBUTORS

Reg Bailey is the Chief Executive of the Mothers' Union, an international organisation with over one million members in 70 countries around the world. The Mothers' Union aims to share the love of Christ by encouraging, strengthening and supporting marriage and family life. Reg is the first man to have held this post, although many men are members of the organisation. Married with an adult son and daughter, Reg was previously the Chief Executive of Danish Bacon Company and Del Monte Foods. He is a licensed Reader in the Church of England.

Rev Glennys Bamford was born in the West Riding of Yorkshire. She read Theology at Leeds University and candidated for the Wesley Deaconess Order. She spent five years working in the South Yorkshire coalfield, looking after three churches. After her marriage, Glennys shared life and ministry with her husband in South Wales, London and Burnley. When her two daughters were in their teens she candidated for the ministry and worked in Wolverhampton and Luton. Since retiring in 1997 she has looked after a small church in Wolverhampton, and also works as a volunteer for the Citizens Advice Bureau.

Rev David Beazley studied at Durham University before teaching Geography in a Comprehensive School for 13 years. After attending Spurgeon's Bible College he became Minister of two churches in West London, now a united and growing Ecumenical Partnership of Baptist and United Reformed Church. He has been involved with The Leprosy Mission for 10 years, on the National and International Councils, and is Chairman of the Council of The Leprosy Mission England, Wales, the Channel Islands and the Isle of Man.

Rev Francis Dewar was a reluctant ordinand in 1960. During his time as an Anglican parish priest he reflected long and hard about vocation. Is it just for clergy? Is it always unwelcome? Is it only to do with paid work? Could it be something you love to do? In 1981 he resigned from parish ministry to start Journey Inward Journey Outward, a registered charity, which is about vocation for everyone. His books include *Live for a Change – discovering and using your gifts* (2nd ed. DLT 1999), *Invitations – God's calling for everyone* (SPCK 1996), *Called or Collared – An alternative approach to vocation* (2nd ed. SPCK 2000) and *Give Yourself a Break* (Hunt & Thorpe 1992).

Hilary Faith Jones grew up in a Methodist household, surrounded by the stories of the Bible and the witness of the present day. This has had a profound effect on her love for people – and her love for God. After training as a musician and actor, she set up her own business as a professional storyteller of world religions within primary schools, a job which she finds immensely fulfilling and rewarding. Hilary is the author of *Awakenings* (also available on cassette) and *Waiting for Jesus*, and is about to publish her first children's book, *The Wonderful Picnic*. All her books are published by The Leprosy Mission. Hilary is a Methodist local preacher in the Nottingham South Circuit.

Rev Harold Good, OBE has been President of the Methodist Church in Ireland, 2001-2002. As well as serving in circuits in both parts of Ireland he has served and studied in the USA. He is a member of the Northern Ireland Human Rights Commission, and a former Chairman of NIACRO (Northern Ireland Association for the Care and Resettlement of Offenders). The former Director of the Corrymeela Centre for Reconciliation, he is also a Board member of *Healing through Remembering*, a project which is currently examining the case for a process of truth and reconciliation in Northern Ireland. Harold Good and his wife, Clodagh, have five children and 10 grandchildren.

Angela Griffiths is a freelance writer who lives in Somerset. Her published work includes fiction and non-fiction for children, and prayers and devotional material for adults. She has written nine books for young adults with reading difficulties. She has also written for radio. Angela was the first 'Encourager' for members of the Association of Christian Writers. She enjoys helping and encouraging people generally.

Linda Hernandez joined the staff of the Methodist Publishing House in 1992 and has been the DISCIPLE Co-ordinator since 1996. Linda readily shares with people how her own faith was deepened and strengthened through taking part in a DISCIPLE Bible study group.

Rev Albert Jewell retired as Senior Chaplain with MHA Care Group (Methodist Homes) in summer 2001 and is presently researching how people cope in 'the fourth age'. He is the author of *Grow Old Along with Me* (NCEC 2001), *Spirituality and Ageing* (Jessica Kingsley 1999) and *Older People and the Church* (MPH 2001). He previously served in a variety of Methodist circuits and as a school and university chaplain. He now lives in Leeds, is married to Gill and rejoices in two children and four grandchildren.

Rt Rev Dr Michael Nazir-Ali was appointed Bishop of Rochester in 1994. He holds both British and Pakistani citizenship, and is the first non-white Diocesan Bishop in the Church of England. From 1989-1994 he was the General Secretary of CMS. His interests have led him to research and study in several fields, including comparative literature, comparative philosophy and theology at the Universities of Cambridge, Oxford, and the Australian College of Theology. He has taught at universities in the UK and in Pakistan, is a Fellow of St. Edmund Hall, Oxford, and visiting Professor of Theology and Religious Studies in the University of Greenwich. Michael Nazir-Ali is the author of seven books and of numerous articles on Mission, Ecumenism, the Anglican Communion, and relations with people of other faiths, particularly Islam.

Rachel Newton is currently Chair of Creative Arts in Methodism, promoting the use of the arts in worship, and has just given up being a member of the editorial team of the Methodist magazine, *Magnet*. She has always been passionately fond of the theatre, trained in drama, and has taught, produced and performed in schools and churches. For the last 11 years of her teaching career, she taught disturbed teenagers in London and Liverpool. Rachel has recently been appointed part-time Chaplain at Wesley College, Bristol, and is a founder member of the Bristol Spirituality Group. Serving as a trustee of The New Room in Bristol, she has researched and helped to furnish the heritage rooms and garden of Charles Wesley's House, now open to the public.

Rt Hon Andy Reed MP is the Labour and Co-operative MP for Loughborough, and Chair of the Parliamentary Christian Fellowship. Before becoming an MP in 1997 Andy was employed by Leicestershire County Council, and previously he also served in a number of other posts in local government. In the House of Commons he has been active in promoting the principles of co-operation locally and nationally, particularly in the field of economic development; he believes that ethical consumerism will play a vital role in the future. His other interests include the Christian Socialist Movement and Amnesty International; he is a keen sportsman, and is President of Loughborough FC and Birstall RFC.

Chief Rabbi Professor Jonathan Sacks has been Chief Rabbi of the United Hebrew Congregations of the Commonwealth since September 1991. At the time of his appointment he was Principal of Jews' College, London, the world's oldest rabbinical seminary, where he also held the Chair in Modern Jewish Thought and instituted novel programmes in rabbinic pre- and in-service training. He has been rabbi of the Golders Green and Marble Arch Synagogues in London. In September 2001, the Archbishop of Canterbury, the Rt Hon Rev George Carey, conferred on the Chief Rabbi a doctorate of Divinity in recognition of the Chief Rabbi's 10 years in the Chief Rabbinate. A gifted communicator, the Chief Rabbi is a frequent contributor to radio, television and the national press – he has a monthly 'Credo' column in *The Times*. He is the author of 12 books, the most recent being *The Politics of Hope: New Revised Edition* (2000), *Celebrating Life* (2000) and *Radical Then Radical Now* (2001).

Rev Briant Smith is a biologist by training, and has always been drawn to the natural environment. For many years he taught sciences, including rural science and environmental education. His first 'encounter with God' was through the beauty of the early morning countryside on the Isle of Wight when he was 20, and ever since then a significant part of his personal journey of faith has been searching for the Creator in the natural beauty which surrounds us. As a Methodist minister Briant has served, and continued his quest, in Southampton, De Gwynedd, and in the West Wight Circuit, where he is currently Superintendent Minister.

Tom Taylor was born in Bury, Lancashire, in 1922. During his childhood he attended Bolton Road Methodist Sunday School from where he had many happy memories. After leaving school Tom worked as an apprentice printer for the *Bury Times*. At the age of 17 he enlisted in the Army and served in Gibraltar, India and Burma, where he was wounded. He returned to England where he trained as a poultry farmer at St Dunstan's, and finally set up his own poultry farm near Leyland. He and his wife, Nancey, had two children, Paul (who is a Methodist minister) and Susan (who died in 2000). Tom became a Methodist local preacher in 1954. When The Open University was established Tom gained a BA (Hons) followed by an MSc at Lancaster University. He was the author of *Through the Hole in My Head* (Foundery Press).

Tom was a man of great courage, determination and faith.

Rev Tony Trevithick was born in Scotland, where his father was an English Methodist minister. He was educated at Kingswood Methodist Boarding School in Bath. While working in a steel works he received a call to the ministry, and after training at Richmond College he was ordained in 1963. He and his wife, Margaret, have two children and three grandchildren. Tony has served as a minister for 42 years, and has recently retired to Worthing.

Esther de Waal is an Anglican lay woman who lives on the borders of England and Wales, in the countryside where she grew up. A sense of place has always been important to her and, after Cambridge, she became the first research student in the newly-founded Department of Local History at Leicester. It was the buildings and their settings in the landscape that led to her interest in monastic spirituality, especially the Benedictine, Cistercian and Celtic traditions, on which she has written extensively. Esther de Waal travels widely and leads retreats in many parts of the world, feeling a particular connection with South Africa. Her home life centres on the 'spirituality' found in her garden and her increasing number of grandchildren.

Sister Eluned Williams spent all her working life with the National Children's Home, for much of the time as Superintendent of the residential children's home in Dinas Powys. She was an embarrassed subject of Michael Aspel's *This is your Life*, and was awarded the MBE for services to child care. Her love for her home country is very apparent – English is her second language. She was Vice-President of the Methodist Conference 2000-2001, and is currently President of Y Gymanfa (The Assembly) for Methodism in Wales. She is also a President of Churches Together in Britain and Ireland.

Fr Abbot Timothy Wright OSB is the Abbot of Ampleforth. Before his election in 1997 he was Deputy Head and Housemaster of Ampleforth College, where he previously taught Geography and Religious Studies. In the early years of GSCE he was involved in developing syllabuses for the Midland Examination Group; this work extended to working for other examination boards at GCSE and A levels. As Abbot he is responsible not only for the Community at Ampleforth but also for its 13 parishes in the north of England, St. Benet's Hall in Oxford, and a small foundation in Zimbabwe. He has co-authored the recently published *Doing Business with Benedict*, which developed from courses at Ampleforth for people interested in applying the Rule of St. Benedict in business life.

ACKNOWLEDGEMENTS

Methodist Publishing House gratefully acknowledges the use of copyright items. Every effort has been made to trace copyright owners, but where we have been unsuccessful we would welcome information which would enable us to make appropriate acknowledgement in any reprint.

Scripture quotations, unless otherwise stated, are from the New Revised Standard Version of the Bible, copyright 1989 by the Division of Christian Education of the National Council of Churches of Christ in the USA.

Page

8   James Jones, *People of the Blessing*, Bible Reading Fellowship.

8   H. Wheeler Robinson, *History of Israel*, Duckworth.

9   Michael Ball, 'Amazing Grace', from *Glimpses in Faith*, ed. Stephen Dawes, Southleigh Publications.

16 Catherine Marshall, *Something More*, Hodder & Stoughton.

18 Eric Milner-White, *My God, My Glory*, by permission of the Friends of York Minster.

19 Kenneth Slack, *New Light on Old Songs*, SCM Press.

20 Flora Slosson Wuellner, *Heart of Healing, Heart of Light*, Upper Room Books, 1992.

21	Thomas Merton, *Conjectures of a Guilty Bystander*, 2nd edn., Sheldon Press, 1977.
26-27	Psalm quotations from *Common Worship*, © *The Archbishops' Council 2000*, Church House Publishing.
31	J. B. Phillips, *Plain Christianity*, Epworth Press.
32	Muriel Stuart, 'The Seed Shop' from *Selected Poems*, by permission of E. A. S. Stapleforth.
39	Anthony Hulbert, *Contours of God*, The Canterbury Press.
40	Thomas R. Hawkins, *The Unsuspected Power of the Psalms*, Upper Room Books, 1985.
40	Simone Weil, *Waiting on God*, Routledge & Kegan Paul.
41	David Adam, 'I weave a silence', from *The Edge of Glory*, SPCK.
41	Wifred Easton, 'God's way of redemption', *Preacher's Handbook 3*, Epworth Press.
42	Cecily Taylor, 'Thank God for tears', *Liturgy of Life*, NCEC. Permission applied for.
49	A. Victor Murray, *Personal Experiences and the Historic Faith*, Epworth Press.
49	H. F. Woodhouse, *Church Quarterly Review*, Oct-Dec 1966.
51	*Rule for a New Brother*, published and copyright by Darton, Longman & Todd Limited, and used by permission of the publishers.

52	'E. M.', a Nun of Burnham Abbey, from *A Book of Faith*, comp. Elizabeth Goudge, Hodder & Stoughton.
59	Elizabeth Jennings, 'Let me learn the quiet of the evergreens', from *Tributes*, Carcanet.
60	Rita F. Snowden, *Sung in our Hearts*, Epworth Press.
68	George Appleton, *The Quiet Heart*, Fount.
69	Betsy Schwarzentraub, *Disciplines*, 16th March 1995, Upper Room Books. Permission applied for.
70	P. F. Holland, 'The means of grace', *Preacher's Handbook 3*, Epworth Press.
71	John S. Hoyland, *Hodder Book of Christian Prayers* 981, Hodder & Stoughton.
80	John Polkinghorne, *Searching for Truth*, Bible Reading Fellowship.
82	'I wait patiently for God' from *Psalms of patience, protest and praise'*, John L. Bell, © 1993, The Iona Community/Wild Goose Publications, Glasgow G2 3DH. Permission applied for.
83	'Faithful One' (chorus) words and music Brian Doerksen, in *Complete Mission Praise*, No 825 © 1989 Mercy/Vineyard Publishing ad. CopyCare, P.O. Box 77, Hailsham BN27 3EF. Permission applied for.
85	W. E. Farndale, *The Psalms in a New Light*, Epworth Press.
87	P. T. R. Kirk, *The Best Book in the World*, Epworth Press.
87	William Barclay, *The Apostles Creed*, Arthur James.

88	John Baillie, *A Diary of Private Prayer*, OUP. Permission applied for.
89	Corrymeela Community Prayer, *Celebrating Together*, Corrymeela Press. Permission applied for.
94	Elizabeth Craven, from Leslie Weatherhead, *A Private House of Prayer* and Morris Maddocks, *A Healing House of Prayer*, Hodder & Stoughton.
95	William Temple, *Readings in St. John's Gospel*, Macmillan.
96	*Forms of Prayer for Jewish Worship: Daily Sabbath & Occasional Prayers* (1977), The Reform Synagogue of Great Britain. Permission applied for.
97-98	Angela Morgan, 'Kinship' from *The Hour has Struck*, (1914), Dodd, Mead & Co., Inc.
105	Pope John Paul II, from *Prayers for Pilgrims*, John Johansen-Berg, published and copyright 1993 by Darton, Longman & Todd Limited, and used by permission of the publishers.
106	Sheila Cassidy, 'Heaven and Hell', *Epworth Review*, Jan. 1993, MPH.
108	James A. Harnish, *Journeys with the People of Genesis*, Upper Room Books.
108	Albert Schweitzer, *Memoirs of Childhood and Youth*, George Allen & Unwin.
115	D. P. Thomson, 'His Greatest Hour', *More Sermons I should like to have Preached*, Epworth Press.
124	E. H. Hobday, *One Crowded Hour*, Epworth Press.

124	Fairfields Whitwell, *The Hill of Contentment*, Sharp.
125	Alison Tomlin, *Spirit Level*, MPH.
126	Kathy Galloway, 'God of the spirit of kindness', © 1996 Kathy Galloway, *The Pattern of our Days – Liturgies and resources for worship*, published by Wildgoose Publications, The Iona Community, Glasgow G2 3DH.
127	W. E. Orchard, *The Temple*, J. M. Dent & Sons. Permission applied for.
127	Teresa Hooley, 'How should I fear to die?' from *Selected Poems* by Teresa Hooley, published by Jonathan Cape. Used by permission of The Random House Group Limited.
132	W. E. Sangster & Leslie Davison, *The Pattern of Prayer*, Epworth Press.
141	Stephen Orchard, *All the Glorious Names*, *Prayer Handbook 1989*, NCEC. Permission applied for.
150	Raymond Abba, *Things which Abide*, Epworth Press.
151	Virginia Thesiger, *Spirit Level*, MPH.
160	George Campbell Morgan, 'The Psalm of the Two Ways', *More Sermons I should like to have Preached*, Epworth Press.
160	Kairos Document, Catholic Institute for International Relations and the British Council of Churches.
162	Leslie Church, *The Fourth Homely Year*, Epworth Press.
169	W. E. Sangster, 'How to be Saved', *More Sermons I should like to have Preached*, Epworth Press.

170   J. Neville Ward, *Beyond Tomorrow*, Epworth Press.

171   Leslie Weatherhead, *His Life and Ours*, Hodder & Stoughton.

172   Richard M. Gula, *To Walk Together Again*, Paulist Press.

173   Loretta Girzaitis, *Disciplines*, 16th July 1992, Upper Room Books.

176   Colin Morris, *Starting from Scratch*, Epworth Press.

178   Margaret Isherwood, *The Root of the Matter*, Gollancz.

180   Eric G. Frost, *Down to Earth Religion*, Epworth Press.